an alban institute publication

P9-CQI-262

c. jeff woods

LINCOLN CHRISTIAN COLLEGE AND SEMINARY

user friendly evaluation

improving the work of pastors, programs and laity

LINCOLN CHRISTIAN COLLEGE AND SEMINARY

The Publications Program of The Alban Institute is assisted by a grant from Trinity Church, New York.

Copyright 1995 by The Alban Institute, Inc. All rights reserved.

This material may not be photocopied or reproduced in any way without written permission.

Library of Congress Catalog Number 95-78600
ISBN 1-56699-154-4

CONTENTS

Acknowledgments   v

Introduction   vii

1. What is evaluation?   1

2. Called to Be Different   13

3. Techniques of Evaluation   27

4. A Fill-in-the-Blank Evaluation   38

5. Evaluation and Church Renewal   47

6. Evaluation and Lay Ministry   56

7. Evaluation and Pastoral Ministry   68

8. The Experts Respond to Dilemmas   76

9. Who are we when we are not doing anything?   85

Appendix A   91
Church Distinctiveness Survey

Appendix B   95
Church Renewal Diagnosis Instrument

90457

Appendix C   101
Annual Ministry Goals for Rev. C. Jeff Woods

Notes   105

Bibliography   111

A Road Map for Readers Needing Immediate Help

For help in:

- formulating an identity of your church, turn to chapter 2.
- formulating a broader base than numbers from which to evaluate church growth, turn to chapter 2.
- surveying your membership, turn to chapter 3.
- evaluating a specific program, turn to chapters 3 and 4.
- assessing your current strengths and weaknesses in church renewal, turn to chapter 5.
- evaluating the ministry of the laity in the workplace, church, or community, turn to chapter 6.
- evaluating a pastor or church staff member, turn to chapter 7.
- deciding whether or not to enlist the help of a church consultant, turn to chapter 8.
- encouraging a long-time volunteer to move on to a different ministry, turn to chapter 8.
- deciding whether or not to add a second worship service, turn to chapter 8.
- evaluating a preaching ministry, turn to chapter 8.

ACKNOWLEDGMENTS

I praise God for gifts of ministry and opportunities to use them.

I thank God for my family. My children, Brandon and Kelsey, provided the material for the epilogues. My wife, Kandy, helped me recall many family conversations. I am appreciative of the life-long encouragement of my sister, Cathy.

I am indebted to Paul Light, Roy Oswald, and Jill Hudson for responding to the dilemmas presented in chapter 8. Their responses were on target and insightful.

I am grateful to people who have given me an opportunity to use my evaluation skills, to Gene Ton, executive minister for American Baptist Churches of Indiana, to the Academy of Parish Clergy, and to various school corporations.

I appreciate Celia Hahn for believing in me and granting me opportunities to write for a wider audience. Thanks to Evelyn Bence for applying her editing skills to this manuscript.

INTRODUCTION

"Rev. Thomas, over the past several months, the board of worship has tackled several different worship issues. We have involved more people, created more variety in our music, and enhanced the meaning of the ordinances. For our next topic, we would like to discuss the possibility of a sermon evaluation procedure."

Sermon evaluation?! Panic. No, it's stronger than that. Terror. That's closer. Discombobulation. Still closer. It's like sending Daniel to the lion's den all over again. No, it's worse than even that. The members of the board of worship mean well, but their critical evaluation skills are second to no other board; I would feel like a lion in a den of Daniels!

After several more seconds of anticipatory grief, Rev. Thomas begins to think a bit more rationally. *Maybe the board of worship means well. Could it be that they really want to help? I'm sure every pastor's sermons could improve, including mine. After all, the entire congregation probably evaluates my sermon every Sunday anyway, although covertly. If they just wouldn't compare my sermons to ones they hear at our annual conferences or to people on TV. I would certainly need to have input into the process myself. The thought still petrifies me, but maybe something good could actually come from this suggestion.*

The word *evaluation* gives rise to many disturbing thoughts: *judgment, error, performance.* The words triggered by *evaluation* can cause people to respond negatively or defensively to whatever else is said about evaluation. People view evaluation as a necessary evil. Even though many people are beginning to see the benefits of an evaluation process, most are still uneasy when the word is spoken.

A User Friendly Book

This is a user friendly book about evaluation. First of all, it is user
friendly because no terms or procedures will be introduced that presume
the reader has taken foundational statistical and measurement classes.
The examples, illustrations, and exercises represent tasks that a church
leader, with little or no background in evaluation, can conduct. I have
not assumed that a local church leader can order and evaluate census
track-data for the church neighborhood. Even when technical concepts
such as this are alluded to, the reader will be directed to published ref-
erences and available resources.

Second, it is user friendly because it approaches evaluation from
the premise that all evaluation procedures should be adapted to the
individual or group using them. Each pastor and congregation is called
to be different from all others. This concept makes evaluation user
friendly by showing that comparisons among congregations are irrel-
evant. Each congregation must evaluate itself in light of its own mix of
gifts, background, talents, and opportunities—its own potential.

Third, the book is user friendly by its practical nature. While I believe that all praxes should be guided by good, sound theory, no theory
will be presented that cannot be tried and tested or used as a guiding
principle by the reader. The book is practical, but it also teaches the
reader about the field of evaluation, detailing principles of evaluation
that can be applied to contexts not contained in the book.

Finally, it is indeed a friendly book. Although evaluation can be
scary, this book will constantly lift up the friendly and helpful side of
evaluation.

Overview of Book

The first chapter of the book provides background information regarding the field of evaluation. Many evaluators may not realize that evaluation is a field of study. In this chapter, I will explain the progression of
evaluation models, touching on authors such as Tyler, Stufflebeam,
Stake, Scriven, and Guba. Different evaluation experts have attempted
to organize their evaluation procedures around different issues, finally

arriving at the postulate that every evaluation procedure should be "responsive" to the specific organization.

This concept of responsive evaluation gives rise to chapter 2, which discusses the many ways congregations might differ. This chapter also provides some tools for each congregation to discover its own uniqueness.

Chapter 3 will detail techniques of evaluation subdivided into four categories. (1) Congregational qualitative assessment includes techniques such as interviewing, building a church's saga, and small-group interactions. (2) Congregational quantitative assessment includes "ten great three-by-five-card surveys," pencil and paper surveying, and methods of analyzing the data obtained. (3) The category "gathering easy data" includes a look at finances, mission giving, and organizational charts. (4) "Gathering data with a little more effort" looks at demographics and "evaluating by walking about in the neighborhood."

Chapter 4 guides the reader through an evaluation procedure. I ask the reader to choose a program or event to evaluate prior to reading the chapter. Can you describe the difference between merit and worth? Do you know the difference between formative and summative evaluation? If not, you need to read chapter 4, designed to compel the reader to analyze the background, the results, the side effects, and the tradeoffs related to the program or event chosen.

Chapters 5 through 7 relate evaluation to church renewal, lay ministry, and pastoral ministry, respectively. Chapter 5 presents a holistic philosophy of church renewal, including a self-scoring diagnostic tool for evaluating a congregation's strongest and weakest paths to renewal. Chapter 6 details three distinct types of lay ministry: (1) ministry to members, (2) community ministry, and (3) on-the-job ministry. I also suggest methods for assessing the three types. Chapter 7, on pastoral ministry, will reveal the link between pastoral strengths and congregational strengths and suggest activities such as annual goal setting, long-range planning, and planned continuing education for professional church leaders.

Chapter 8 gives information from three experts in the field of congregational evaluation, asking them to respond to four dilemmas in the field of church evaluation. It is also the reader's opportunity to begin wrestling with the book's insights and information.

Chapter 9 asks the question, "Who are we when we are not doing

anything?" This chapter looks at the times in the life of a congregation
when the corporate body is not gathered together. Here I encourage the
reader to begin developing an "evaluator's eye" in assessing the subtle
messages sent by a church through written communication, informal
conversations, responses to requests, and the social grapevine.

It is not necessary to read the chapters in order. Someone with a
severe pain in the abdomen should not be forced to endure an entire
physical examination prior to receiving relief from that pain. If you
purchased this book for immediate help with a specific situation, refer to
the map at the end of the table of contents for directions on where to find
prompt assistance for your predicament.

But once a person's abdominal pain has subsided, the physician will
usually initiate a more detailed search for the root causes of the pain in
hopes that the pain will not reoccur. Once you have received help for
your specific situation, you might benefit by learning some of the
broader preventative principles of evaluation. Once you are out of the
crisis, why not read the entire book to gain a more ample perspective of
evaluation?

The end of each chapter contains a conversation between me and
one of my children. Here my goal is to explain a concept by presenting
common sense insight; you can see that particular concept through the
eyes of a child. My children, Brandon and Kelsey, are now six and eight,
although some of the conversations in the epilogues took place years ago.
The chapter epilogues are one more attempt at being user friendly.

The bibliography contains many evaluation resources for readers
who wish to explore certain issues in more detail. Many researchers and
authors have added significantly to the field of evaluation. Too little is
known of these contributions. While congregations may develop their
own approaches to evaluation, I believe all can benefit from wrestling
with the issues raised by experts in the evaluation field.

The book is guided by four principles of evaluation already alluded
to in this introduction. I list them here for easy reference and to begin
dispelling your fears about this field called evaluation.

1. Why be nervous? Everything ever done is always evaluated
   anyway.

2. Why worry about comparisons? Every evaluation should be
   tailored to the unique characteristics of the organization.

3. Why worry about outcomes? The ultimate goal of evaluation is to improve the situation for all involved.

4. Why worry about choosing a process? No evaluation process is ever fixed in stone.

CHAPTER 1

What is evaluation?

Sunday night. The epilogue to another Sabbath day. *The sermon seemed to go well. We had an average crowd for an end-of-the-summer Sunday. All is going well. Although—we did have more last Sunday than this Sunday. Wait a minute. That doesn't fit. Shouldn't we be steadily increasing as we approach the beginning of the school year?! Even though attendance today was average, why did we have fewer out this Sunday than last Sunday? Maybe I ought to check this week's attendance against a year ago the same Sunday. Maybe I ought to compute a five-year trend analysis for this particular Sunday.*

Let's see, the Thompsons were back. The Fryes were back. Who was still on vacation? What possible reason could there be for attendance being lower this Sunday than last? Maybe people have come home from vacation but are taking another short trip before the summer officially ends. I guess I am not too alarmed. Maybe I should be. Is there some reason people are staying away? I haven't heard anything through the grapevine. Would I? It might depend upon why they were staying away.

Do I go through this every Sunday night? It seems so. I've tried to put these thoughts out of my mind, but they bombard me until I let them have their day in the corners of my mind. Then it's over, on to Monday. I wonder if any other pastor ever stews like this?

Paranoia? No. Very natural thoughts. Everything ever done by anyone is evaluated. Obviously some people are more driven to evaluate their own behavior than others, but everyone engages in self-evaluation to some degree.

We also regularly and surreptitiously evaluate the habits of other people.

Problems occur only when someone publicly evaluates the work of another. When we're on the receiving end of that evaluation, we get nervous.

To alleviate fear of being evaluated unfairly, people spend a great deal of time trying to assure others that a chosen evaluation process will be fair to all involved. Easier said than done. Deciding the most appropriate way to evaluate a program or person is a complex problem. Is it most equitable to evaluate a program by comparing its accomplishments to its designated goals? What about negative side effects? What about unintended favorable outcomes? How would an ingeniously designed but poorly implemented process be evaluated? These questions and similar ones have led to the development of various evaluation models over the years.

Early Years of Evaluation

The field of evaluation actually dates back to 2200 B.C. when the emperor of China instituted competence criteria for his public officials.[1] But the earliest name associated with evaluation is that of Joseph Rice. In the late 1800s Rice devised achievement tests to try to demonstrate an inefficiency in the use of schooltime. The goal of his evaluation process was to proclaim failure so that change could occur. From that time on, and still today, many people associate evaluation with the disclosure of problems. This negative spin is itself a problem.

Too often people do not consider a formal evaluation procedure until a program is perceived to have serious flaws. The motive in such situations? *Let's try to prove that a particular program is not working so that the program may be killed or destroyed.* Words like *destroy* and *kill* understandably have given evaluation a wicked connotation. For many, the term *evaluation* implies a potential death sentence. Setting out on an evaluation with the intent of fine tuning a program did not arise until years later in the development of evaluation procedures.

In addition to linking evaluation to a death sentence, Rice also linked evaluation to measurement. In the primal years, evaluation and measurement became synonymous. The roots of the field of evaluation were firmly grounded in a scientific paradigm with this motto: "To really know something, one must be able to show concrete evidence to support the claim." For years people did not formally evaluate anything that could not be meticulously measured. On the surface, this linkage does not appear to be problematic, even to people today. But consider this question: Has anything important ever emanated from a program that you just couldn't measure? Of course. Sometimes the most notable aspects of a program are not connected to how many people attended an event or to measurable changes in their behavior, but, rather, to subtle shifts in attitude and changes in atmosphere.

Consider this example: After the implementation of a program designed to bring about healing in a congregation, one might say, "Prior to this program, you could cut the tension in this church with a knife. Now people are speaking to one another and actually sounding civil toward one another." Measuring a tense atmosphere or a civil conversation is a difficult task. And in the early years of evaluation, anything that could not be measured was deemed not important. This means that many important contributions of programs, ideas, and people were discounted.

Goals-Based Evaluation

The next major player in the evaluation field did little to alter the assumptions upon which evaluation had been formed—that evaluation involved uncovering problems and measuring activity. Ralph Tyler increased the link between judgment and evaluation by bonding evaluation to objectives.[2] This act strengthened the assumption that the purpose of evaluation was to discover if a particular idea had worked. To discover whether or not objectives had been met, Tyler stated that measurement should be only one device in the evaluator's tool belt. And yet few examples of assessment, other than measuring devices, were actually used by Tyler's proteges.

Using Tyler's Model to Evaluate a Church Program

A congregational example may help illustrate Tyler's model. If a church decided to use Tyler's model in evaluating a discipling program, it would evaluate the program based upon whether or not the goals of the program were achieved. If the goal of the program was to train four disciplers, who in turn would disciple four people each in the coming year, Tyler's model would ask whether or not sixteen people were actually discipled during the year. If another goal of the program was to teach a group of people about the tenets of the particular faith or denomination, evaluators might devise an instrument to measure how much people enrolled in the course actually learned. Ideally, to measure this last objective, Tyler would suggest creating an instrument that measured one's knowledge of the denomination and then administering the same test to people on the opening day of the class and again after the completion of the class, comparing the results.

Problems Develop in Using Tyler's Model

Tyler's model explicitly focused on objectives. This model made great sense on paper, especially to the most rational of thinkers. Strong "thinkers" might ask, "How else would you ever evaluate something, other than according to whether or not the goals of the program were accomplished?" One problem with Tyler's model, however, is with the goals themselves. At the outset of a program, it is extremely difficult to list all the results you hope a program will accomplish. In the end the greatest benefit of a particular program might never have been envisioned from its original design. Additionally, once a program is underway, it is often discovered that one or two of the initial objectives will be impossible to accomplish. Tyler's model did not provide a way to evaluate the objectives themselves and did not provide a way to evaluate anything not tied to an objective.

One example highlighting the flaws of objectives evaluation occurred when the federal government, under Nixon's administration, evaluated Project Headstart. The goal of the program was to help disadvantaged children get a headstart on education. The activities of the program centered on creating a positive atmosphere at home for impoverished children. Workers in the program tried to educate parents on good nutrition, the importance of providing safe and adequate shelter, and so forth. When the program was evaluated, however, it was evaluated against the measurable goal of how well Headstart children performed on standardized academic tests. The results of these tests killed the program for a period of time.

Complex Programs Compound Earlier Problems

In the days following Ralph Tyler, the American public called for accountability of their governmental leaders and demanded evaluation of their programs. As the world became more and more complex, however, problems arose in defining effectiveness and accountability. Early evaluators, tainted by the origins of the field, suffered from methodological myopia. They were trained to look for flaws rather than strengths. Prior to writing the check, funders of programs asked that an evaluation procedure be attached to every program. Of course no program was perfect, especially programs aimed at helping a more and more diverse group of Americans. As problems occurred, program evaluators were equipped with hammers to fix problems that did not require hammers.

Eventually the problems associated with measuring objectives led to the demise of Tyler's model. Following the 1957 launching of Sputnik, American educators launched their own flurry of activity aimed at making America number one again in education. Complex programs, developed during the 1960s, were too enigmatic to be evaluated merely by an objectives model. New programs called for new evaluation methods. The field of education became the training ground not only for new educational methods, but also for new ways to evaluate them. Several authors suggested other means of organizing an evaluation procedure.

Overview of Other Evaluation Models

To continue tracing the roots of the field of evaluation, I will recount three more evaluation models, each one calling for a different means of designing an evaluation procedure. As each model is delineated, I will again show how a church might evaluate a discipling program based upon the proposed procedure. Tyler's model was an objectives model. When people evaluated a program according to Tyler's model, they began and ended by looking at the goals of the program. The next three models base their procedures on a different organizer, other than goals. The three models are built on three different foundations: decisions, effects, and issues.

It is important to note that many evaluation models contain similar procedures; some of the differences between models may be more semantic than substantive. Differing models encourage evaluators to approach evaluation designs differently. But in the end the various models may result in some of the same recommendations and procedures.

Decisions-Based Evaluation

Tyler's goals-based model asks this question: What is the difference between what was stated and what occurred? The evaluator using this model needs information about objectives and outcomes. Conversely, an evaluator using a decisions-based model needs information about what decisions need to be made: Who makes decisions? What is the timeline for decisions? Who gives input? Who is potentially affected by the decisions?

Stufflebeam proposed a decisions-based model for evaluation and conjured up a typology of decision making.[3] A typology is a way of categorizing things. Stufflebeam suggested that in an organization four types of decisions are made. This model is sometimes called the CIPP model, an acronym for the four types of decisions: context, input, process, and product.

Evaluating the Context—Intended Goals

First, people make decisions about the *context* behind the intended outcomes. Context relates to the circumstances and background information that shape the dreams one has for a particular program. Stufflebeam began his model by addressing the black hole contained in Tyler's model, which assumed the preexistence of a program's objectives and goals. Stufflebeam said that people need to analyze a program's context prior to making a decision about its goals.

Apply this first step of Stufflebeam's model to the designing of an evaluation procedure for a discipling program. You might analyze the context surrounding the goals of a discipling program by asking the following probing questions: What outcomes do you desire for your discipling program? What do you want people to know? What parts of the Bible are most important? What is important about your particular denomination? How can people begin to apply what they learn? Should application be one of the goals? Stufflebeam's model encourages leaders to evaluate their context prior to announcing the goals for a particular program.

Evaluating Sources of Input—Intended Means

Stufflebeam's second type of decision involves assessing the *input* required to determine the best means for arriving at the stated goals. Stufflebeam's model alerts leaders to look at the various sources of input available to achieve the goals of a program. The following questions could help a church leader appraise the sources of input for a discipling program: Who should come to a discipling class? New members or inquirers? What ages should be targeted? How should the disciplers be chosen? What materials are currently available from our denomination? What other materials are available? Should the pastor do all of the training or some of the training? Who else should be involved in the leading? Should the program involve other leaders outside the local congregation?

Intended *goals* emerge as one analyzes the context. Intended *means* grow as one analyzes the potential input from various sources. Together, intended goals (context) and intended means (input) make up one-half of Stufflebeam's model. Generally speaking, half of the decisions that affect a program are made prior to the implementation of the program; the other half are made once the program is underway.

Evaluating the Process—Actual Means

Actual goals and means make up the second half of the decision-making process. Evaluating what actually occurred is an evaluation of the *process* that took place. What did happen? Who did come? From where did they come? How was the program actually advertised? Which type of advertising proved to be the most beneficial?

Evaluating the Product—Actual Goals

Evaluating the actual results of a program is an evaluation of the *product*. What are these discipled people like now? Are they different? What are their attitudes toward our church? Our denomination? The Bible? Future learning? What exactly is this product we have created that is known as a discipling program?

Strengths and Weaknesses

Every model contains strengths and weaknesses. Stufflebeam's CIPP model expanded the possible organizers for an evaluation procedure beyond objectives. The model encourages the evaluator to focus not only on actual means and ends, but also on intended means and ends. The faults of the CIPP model center around its assumptions about the role of the decision maker. Who is in charge of a particular decision? Sounds like an easy question to ask. But sometimes an evaluator discovers that within an organization the buck never stops. Additionally, decision makers do not always have access to comprehensive information. A decision maker may report that she would have made an entirely different decision if she could have created a different scenario within the organization. Unfortunately, decision makers are limited to the resources and traditions of their organization, and this reality limits the effectiveness of the CIPP model of evaluation.

Another weakness of the CIPP model involves its failure to take into account the biases of decision makers; decisions are inevitably influenced by personal views and hopes for the organization. Some people who really believe in the cause behind the program may embellish nonmeasurable outcomes. Others, hoping that a program fails so they can put their own program or agenda on the table, may unintentionally or even intentionally alter the outcomes in a negative direction.

Effects-Based Evaluation

This problem of decision-maker bias led Michael Scriven to suggest that programs be evaluated solely upon their effects, with absolutely no attention given to whether or not the goals of the program were achieved.[4] Scriven suggested that the goals of a program be kept secret from the people in the organization. What a radical thought! You're kidding, right? No. Scriven was serious. While many people disagreed with the intent behind the design of Scriven's model, consensus grew around the virtues of the model itself. Scriven proposed the idea of "effects" as an organizer or base for the evaluator. What effects, intended or unintended, did the program actually have? Who cares if the program actually met its goals or not, so long as other unintended side effects of the program were deemed worthy? Scriven proposed the notion of goal-free evaluation. Rather than compare what was achieved to what was intended, Scriven suggested comparing the actual effects to the needs of the people in the organization.

Scriven's model shifted the pendulum away from heavy human control toward a tolerance and even anticipation for the unexpected. This model advocated taking evaluation one step at a time, not rushing ahead of grace. Scriven's model did not involve a simple rearranging of the deck chairs. It steered the ship in a whole new direction.

Evaluating Expected Effects

Let's apply Scriven's model to the evaluation of a discipling program. Within any discipling program, some needs will be universal. People have a need to know the basic tenets of the faith. People have a need to know how to study the Bible. People have a need to understand the different components of a mature Christian life. According to an effects-based evaluation, a discipling program that helped to meet these needs would be deemed effective, regardless of how many people actually attended or whether or not the original goals were met.

Evaluating Unexpected Effects

Scriven's model added a new dimension to evaluation. Since "effects" are the only evaluation criteria of this model, this model encourages evaluators to scrutinize very carefully unintended outcomes.

Using an effects-based model, a discipling program could be graded with an "A," even if it failed to meet all intended outcomes but did meet needs that one never thought a discipling program could address. Consider this scenario. Suppose that very few of the people involved in a recent discipling program came away with their needs met in the traditional areas—understanding the tenets of their faith, having a mature Christian life, and knowing how to study the Bible. Suppose that much of the group discussion time had centered around members' daily lives and that the discipling group subsequently formed into a support group. This effects-based model is the first we've discussed that would evaluate positively this discipling program. Most people have a need for a support group. They may still need discipling, but Scriven's model would evaluate this particular discipling program as being effective because it met certain needs of the participants.

Consider one more similar example of a positive effects-based evaluation. Suppose that a second discipling program did little to teach people the basic tenets of the faith. The weekly program went off on obscure tangents, leaving little time to focus on the designed curriculum. But suppose it did instill in the participants a strong desire to learn more. An evaluation that asked what the effects of the program were, regardless of whether objectives were met, would uncover that this "extra" need had been met: People have a need to hunger and thirst for more learning. Any program that met that need, intended or not, would be viewed as successful under an effects-based evaluation.

Response-Based Evaluation

An examination of Scriven's model raises two important considerations in evaluation: (1) Shouldn't an evaluation process uncover what is most important? (2) Won't "what is most important" depend on the unique characteristics of each organization?

Such questions lead us to a fourth type of evaluation model, called the responsive model. A responsive model is one that attempts to uncover the most important issues of a program and then evaluate people and programs in light of those issues. This model asks an evaluator to gain familiarity with the program before deciding which questions to ask and what data to gather. The responsive model asks "What do people already think about this program?" to understand how people may be filtering the purposes of the program.

Defining Response-Based Evaluation

Stake was the first to suggest a responsive model of evaluation.[5] He suggested that one observe a program and only then determine what to look for. According to Stake, steps for a responsive evaluation procedure should include:

1. Talking with the clients and program staff to gain a sense of their posture.
2. Placing limits on the scope of the program.
3. By observation, beginning to discover the purposes of the program.
4. Conceptualizing the problems and issues that the evaluation should address.
5. Designing the evaluation around the issues discovered.
6. Gathering data according to the design.
7. Looking for broad themes in the gathered data.
8. Organizing the format for the report.
9. Presenting findings and recommendations to the organization.

Expanding Response-Based Evaluation

The responsive model assesses biases to understand how outcomes may have been altered by the people within the organization. For anyone considering the responsive model, I suggest an expansion of the model. Any program within an organization should not be evaluated only in light of the existing biases of the evaluators and important aspects of the program. Rather, a responsive evaluation should be responsive to the entire organization! This means a responsive evaluation must include an examination of the values and qualities of the entire organization. Such an examination helps determine whether or not the important characteristics of the organization are being promoted by its leaders and programs. An evaluation process should be responsive not only to the character of the program or person being evaluated, but also to the character of the entire organization. In my mind, the ultimate goal of responsive evaluation should ask, "Is this program or person continuing to advance the essence of who we are as an organization?"

Reconsider the example mentioned above regarding the discipling program that did little to propagate the basic tenets of the faith, but effectively created a support group among the participants. The effects-based model helped us to see that side effects can be extremely important. But the responsive model takes us one step further in comparing the total effects of a program to the unique character of an organization. Evaluating the worth of the support group formed by the discipling group would be dependent upon the characteristics of the church in which the support group formed. This discipling program would probably be viewed as much more effective for a church organized around cell groups than for a church known for its prophetic stands.

Ultimately, an evaluation process should be responsive to the particular organization in which the evaluation is conducted. But this means that one must know one's own church. That task, addressed in chapter 2, may sound easy, but it probably is not.

But, first, the epilogue to chapter 1. The epilogue to each chapter is a conversation between me and one of my children, as I attempt to further explain one of the concepts addressed in the chapter.

The Epilogue

A few years ago, our newspaper began including a full-color picture on the front page. Often the picture has nothing to do with the cover story but simply attracts the eye. One day the newspaper printed a beautiful picture of several animals in the wild. It amazed me how the photographer had captured so many different animals in one shot on film. My son took one look at the picture and replied, "Who let them out?"

He had been to the zoo several times. The people who had taken him to the zoo had never thought to explain how the zoo animals got there, where they came from, or why each type was housed in a different environment.

For me this illustrated that we can evaluate only according to our history. For many, the entire extent of their evaluation world lies in asking, "Did this program or person accomplish what was intended?" Evaluation can be so much more than that. Read on to find out how new evaluation principles and tools can open up a whole new world for you.

CHAPTER 2

Called to Be Different

I consistently dread the first few moments of every annual conference held for the pastors in my district. An inhumane custom calls for the meeting to be held the week after Easter, so those who had jumbo-sized Easter crowds and boastable baptisms can prey on those who did not. While the scramble format for the golf tourney is always scheduled the following day, the real shotgun start takes place in the foyer prior to the first plenary. Pastors arrange themselves in different corners of the room and, at a predestined time, begin firing away at one another, loaded with their attendance figures.

One year a wise friend told me that he always avoids the first few minutes of the first plenary session. That was a clever thought, but it might mean missing the announcement of where to find the ice cream social after the meeting, which tee to arrive at the next day, or what time to line up for breakfast.

Another friend told me that she always adds worship and Sunday school attendance figures together when responding to point-blank inquisitors who ask, "And how many did you have last Sunday?" She has found this more effective than merely exaggerating and qualifying the exaggeration with the pet phrase *ministerially speaking.*

The only kind thing about the opening mingle session is that the slaughter does not last long. Those with the large crowds can't hold it in any longer than a few nanoseconds.

Toward a New Model of Measuring Success

The church still has a problem judging success by means other than numbers. I suppose a primary reason for this is that there once was a time when nearly every church grew numerically each year. That was also in an age when it did not matter much what the church did. The people still came. A person in our church remarked recently about a similar phenomenon in business. "There was a time when someone could make a bunch of mistakes and still succeed in a small business. Today, only business people survive in business." Gone are the days when every year every pastor seemed to have more this Easter than last Easter. People have always come to church in response to great programming, creative worship, and real opportunities for fellowship. But gone are the days when people will still come to church in spite of what the church or its leadership does.

The Changing Climate

The climate has changed. I do not think that pastors work less hard today than they did thirty years ago. I contend that the major influences in the decline of church attendance are related to a changing society. The American public is not as supportive of church as it once was. Loren Mead has revealed how today's church is operating in a transitional paradigm, one in which the environment is becoming less and less sympathetic toward the church.[1] To be sure, the church has contributed to this lack of confidence. At times, it has ignored the needs of people in closest proximity to the church building, created scandals among its leaders, and unknowingly erected barriers to particular generations. But even though pastors and congregations may have contributed to the declines in church attendance, this "contribution" should not elicit 100 percent of the blame. Many pastors today have blamed themselves for a decline that is not solely their fault.

People making decisions about whether or not to attend church have been influenced by a variety of other factors besides clergy behavior. People have more choices to occupy their time. Many people have sought out spiritual help from places other than the local church. Many people are fed up with institutions in general. Even when the work of the pastor is rated very positively by a congregant, the work of the pastor is probably not the determining factor in a person's initial decision—whether or not to attend or join a church.

People used to come to church because it was the thing to do. A previous generation held to a motto: We were there every time the church doors were open. Getting those kinds of people in church didn't require a great deal of creative programming. Very few evangelism programs did not work. People came to church because society believed in church.

That is no longer true. Today some evangelistic programs succeed, while others clearly fail. Churches have also discovered a multitude of other worthy programs that are not overtly evangelistic. While many programs can become entry points for a congregation, not every program is intended to lead to increased numbers. Some are meant to lead to other kinds of successes. This means that evaluation aimed primarily at measuring numbers is not helpful to the pastoral leadership or the congregation.

More Than Numbers

Some churches are beginning to measure success by means other than numbers as a result of applying the ideas from Loren Mead's book *More Than Numbers: The Ways Churches Grow.*[2] Mead points out that churches grow in at least three ways besides numerically: (1) *Maturational growth*—in the stature and maturity of each member. (2) *Organic growth*—of the congregation as a functional community. (3) *Incarnational growth*—in the congregation's ability to enflesh in the community what the faith is all about.

If these titles intrigue you, I encourage you to look at Mead's book as a resource for communicating holistic growth to your congregation. Chances are, you are already promoting several kinds of growth in your congregation, but you might have lacked the language to communicate a comprehensive growth model to others in your congregation.

Pastors have been promoting maturational, organic, and incarnational growth for a very long time. But in previous years, nearly every congregation was also getting bigger, so no one complained about measuring success by numbers. Only when the numbers started to decline did

---

churches realize that measuring success solely by numbers was probably never a very good idea in the first place.

Just as there are a variety of ways in which to grow, there are a multitude of potentials for each type of growth. Just as the potential for numerical growth is different for each congregation, the potential for unity, maturity, or ministry will be influenced by the specific nature of each congregation. A later section in this chapter will help you ponder your church's potential.

A Hard Habit to Break

Though most churches now intuitively know that success should be broader than numbers, this numerical evaluation is a hard habit to break; all church traditions are hard to break. Have you heard how many church members it takes to change a light bulb? Four. One to install and three to talk about how much better the old light bulb really was. People in churches like to hold on to old ways of doing things, whether it be styles of worship, methods of evangelism, or measuring success. People and pastors in numerically growing churches often cannot resist the temptation to impose the old model of measuring success on other churches that choose to grow in alternative ways. All of the ways in which churches grow are important. I believe equally important.

Because the needs of people have changed dramatically in recent years, it is essential that our churches begin to evaluate on the basis of their own uniqueness. I repeat: People will no longer come just because the doors are open. This means a church must offer programs that match the needs of the people in the community and the church's own capabilities. The success of a particular program must be calibrated by more sophisticated techniques than merely answering "How many came?"

New Criteria for Evaluating Success

I propose a new model for measuring success based upon two criteria; the ultimate measures of success for any specific aspect of the church should be: (1) How much did this aspect improve the situation for all involved? and (2) How much did this aspect advance our church's overall mission?

A variety of techniques may be employed to discover how much an event improved a situation. The next chapter will present several of these techniques. But no number of procedures can reveal whether or not an event advanced a church's mission if the church does not know its mission! To evaluate whether a specific feature of a church championed that church's future, the church must fully understand who it is and where it is headed.

Every Church Is Unique

No other church is exactly like yours. No other congregation has had the same pastoral leadership, membership, founding ancestors, struggles, crises, celebrations, or soul. Each of these characteristics influences who you are as a church today. Many people interpret Paul's analogy of the church as the body of Christ, in 1 Corinthians 11, as a comparison between each individual church member and each body part. By forming the analogy in this way, the body is represented by one local church.

I believe that the passage may also be read as a comparison between each individual congregation and each body part. By forming the analogy in this second way, the body is then represented by a collection of local churches.

Each local church within a community will often perform one distinct aspect of God's comprehensive mission in a unique and powerful way. It probably would not take you long to think of an extremely evangelistic congregation in your community. How about a discipling church? How about a church known for reaching out into the community? A church that does a great job of ministering to its own membership? Together, the churches in a community form a body analogous to the body of Christ. Not every church is called to be all things to all people. The image of Christ takes on many different manifestations according to the demeanor of each specific congregation.

Function is one of the most visible ways that churches in a community differ. But there are a host of other differences. I will explore three more ways in which all churches differ as further testimony to the uniqueness of each congregation and as a means of encouraging readers to begin formulating the distinctiveness of their church. Then I will present more detailed ways to discover a church's identity.

Differing Histories

First, consider that each church has its own unique *history*. Churches
differ because no two churches travel the same path through time. To
help discover the historic path of your church, ponder the church's saga
as expressed through congregational stories. Historical events in the life
of a congregation shape the future identity of that congregation. What
events have shaped your church's saga? Ask. It will not take long to
discover what people recall in your church's history. One or two significant elements often emerge. A social issues struggle, a move to a new
location, a community ministry, the firing of a pastor, a scandalous situation, or the tenure of an influential pastor—all are events that shape the
collective character of a congregation.

   Two churches similar in size, location, and doctrine may differ
greatly because of the individual sagas, elements in the formation of
their identities. One may have had pastorates averaging three years in
length; the other church might have averaged eight years. That would
make a difference in the personalities of the two congregations. One
may have lived through a fire. The other may have lived through a building program. One may have been started centuries ago by people looking for religious freedom. The other may have been planted by a neighboring church. Past congregational stories bear upon future decisions
and influence the kinds of ministries that a church can perform.

Differing Climates

Congregational climate is a second phenomenon that shapes a local
church's identity. Factors that sway a church's climate include the size
of the congregation, the shape of the sanctuary, the way each member
assumes responsibility, the way the church rewards its members, the
number of risks taken, the amount of warmth and support felt by members, and the degree of tolerance a congregation shows to its members.
Does your church already have a motto? What does that motto say about
your climate? If you were asked to relate your congregation to an animal,
what would it be? What song captures the essence of who you are as a
church? How do people usually feel after a worship service at your
church? Reflection techniques such as these can help a church initially
focus on its unique climate.

Mead writes, "Churches seem to have personalities. I mean local congregations, the ones we sometimes call parishes or congregations."[3] The personality of a congregation forms a part of its climate. To help identify one's climate for ministry, you might also focus on a typology of church personalities. Through extensive survey research and naturalistic inquiry, Carl Dudley and Sally Johnson[4] identified five types of congregational personalities:

1. *The pillar church*—churches that offer the entire community a source of strength, stability, and religious vision.
2. *The pilgrim church*—churches rooted in a people and a tradition, often founded by immigrants and arising out of cultural enclaves.
3. *The survivor church*—churches, often located in declining neighborhoods, that continue to minister to the needs around them in the best way they know how.
4. *The prophet church*—churches that are assertive, restless, and ready to risk all for their vision of God's reign.
5. *The servant church*—churches that respond to individuals—whoever they are and whatever they need.

Differing Environments

Environmental factors are a third phenomenon contributing to the uniqueness of a congregation. Environmental factors are components that influence your church from the outside. They include your church's location, relationships with community agencies, the type of housing in the neighborhood, traffic patterns, weather patterns, and stability factors. A church in a transitional neighborhood and a church in suburbia will perform radically different tasks as they realistically seek to meet the needs of their members and the people in their neighborhoods. So will two churches located in two small towns affected by vastly differing industry. A church down an obscure side-street may have dramatically different opportunities for advertising than one on a corner lot.

Together, history, climate, and environment have a huge influence on the type of ministries a church can tackle. That reality is both wonderful and disturbing. It is disturbing because it suggests that some ministries, performed very successfully in other churches, may not be appropriate for your congregation. It is wonderful because it also suggests that your church is in an exceptional position to perform certain ministries that no one else can accomplish.

Being Unique Is Wonderful

These differences breathe life into the uniqueness of each congregation. A church may be tempted to look at another congregation bolstered by many opportunities for evangelism—by virtue of its saga, its climate, and its environment—and cry, "Foul!" But such a cry ignores the opportunities uniquely present in that congregation. Carrying out God's mission means much more than taking advantage of opportunities to grow in size. Being unique, every congregation is able to perform a particular ministry or set of ministries better than any other congregation.

It never fails: When a church takes time to discover its uniqueness, ministry opportunities and resources seem to jump to the fore.

Where to start? The easiest place to discover ministry opportunities as they are connected to church identity is through environmental factors. An analysis of one's neighborhood quickly leads a church to new possibilities—linking environmental factors with ministry opportunities. Is your church ministering to the senior-adult complex nearby? Is it providing an after-school program for the latch-key children in your neighborhood? What will your church do about the lack of community parking space identified through your analysis? How may your church parking space be used by people in your community through the week? How might your church building be used?

Environmental analyses and ministry opportunities are easily connected. But don't stop there. An assessment of your church's unique background and climate can also give rise to possible ministries. Second Corinthians 1:3-4 suggests that having had a particular experience enables someone to console someone else going through similar circumstances with the same encouragement that God once provided to the ministering party. It is the same for churches and groups of people within a church. What ministries might your church easily perform based upon the events in its saga? A church that has survived a natural disaster possesses a strength for ministry unlike many other congregations. A church with a thirty-year senior pastorate as a part of its saga will possess both opportunities and limitations unique to this circumstance.

Ministries can also flow naturally out of an examination of one's climate. Is your climate naturally one of openness and flexibility? Or of strong organization? What ministries will such a climate enable you to perform? Certain ministries, such as singles' ministries and alternative worship services, thrive in creative climates; others, such as day-care centers and caregivers' day-out programs, need a strong stable base from which to operate. What is God calling your church to do that will be easier for you than any other church, based upon who you are?

Further Help in Discovering Your Church's Identity

As stated earlier, one goal of evaluation is to assess a person, event, or program based on whether or not the person or program has advanced the particular mission of that congregation. But a congregation must know its identity before it can compare the effects of a program or ministry of a person to its overall hopes and dreams.

Once a church has been convinced of its uniqueness, it can institute any number of procedures aimed at discovering the portrait of its uniqueness. Unfortunately, many of the tools available to help a church discover its identity do not help a congregation discover its true distinctiveness. Discovering one's identity and discovering one's unique identity are often two different tasks. For example, nearly every congregation could claim the following phrase as part of its mission statement: "We are a congregation committed to evangelism, discipling, and meeting the needs of people in our congregation, our community, and the world, by exercising our spiritual gifts." That statement might reveal something about a church's identity, but it would do little to show how one particular congregation differs from all other congregations.

Every congregation should ask, "What makes us different from every other congregation?" Ponder and discuss the answer.

What Makes This Survey Different

Additionally, your church may wish to take a survey designed to discover your distinctiveness. Many instruments fail to uncover distinctions because their survey categories are too broad or too narrow. But through the use of statistical procedures, I have designed an instrument that can reveal what makes your church different from others. I admit the initial motivation for designing the survey was rather selfish. I wanted to know what made my church distinct. I wanted to know how our church's worship service, church school program, and decision-making structure differed from others. To do this properly, I had to conduct two studies.

How This Survey Was Designed

I began with a fifty-item survey allowing people to rate what they value about their church; possibilities included reaching the unchurched, co-operating with other churches, enlisting members' financial support, having children's sermons, and so forth. People from several churches were asked to rate the importance of each item. This initial questionnaire served to reduce the number of items on the final questionnaire.

To reduce a long survey to a smaller one, I combined items into categories by a statistical process known as factor analysis. The process works as follows: Items that are consistently similarly rated are grouped together. For example, if every person who rates item 4 low also rates item 7 low, and every person who rates item 4 high also rates item 7 high, then we might conclude that items 4 and 7 are not really measuring anything different. With this procedure I was able to reduce the fifty items on the original survey to nine independent categories—nine "dimensions of church distinctiveness."

If I had begun by listing several broad categories myself, rather than allowing the respondents to form the categories by their ratings, I would never have been able to produce independent categories; the independent nature of the categories in a survey allows a congregation to discover how it differs from another congregation.

When a church ranks these nine independent dimensions according to importance, it discovers what makes it different from other churches. You can find the Church Distinctiveness Survey in appendix A.[5]

Labeling the independent categories or dimensions is the most fruitful and difficult aspect of a factor analysis. For example, after reviewing the results of the initial survey, I discovered that one set of items consistently ranked together included these phrases: "showing love and care for our members"; "hospital visitation"; "family camping"; "counseling"; "ministering to people in crisis"; and "church-wide dinners." I thought I had made a coding error and checked the raw data several times. Content that a figuring error had not been made, I finally began to ask what these seemingly diverse items could have in common and realized that each one dealt with a ministry to a church's own membership. So I labeled one of the dimensions on the final survey "ministry to members."

Another set of items that respondents grouped together on the initial survey included almost every aspect of worship except the sermon! The sermon they connected to items such as Bible study, vacation Bible school, Sunday school teacher training, and mission awareness. I labeled the first of these two factors "adoration" and the other the "cognitive" dimension of church distinctiveness.

Using the Survey

When our church took the final survey of church distinctiveness, the results revealed several important facets of our identity. Collectively, our church rated adoration as most important. I knew the congregation had a keen awareness of the worshipful aspect of the Sunday morning service, but I had not expected this dimension to be number one. With Passion Week soon approaching, I immediately put this new piece of information to the test. Our tradition called for two extra sermons from the pastor during Passion Week. Instead of sermons, I designed two highly participative and experiential services. These two services elicited more positive comments than had any other services during the year. Since that initial discovery, our church has continued to emphasize participative and creative worship, once hosting a series of experiential worship services and annually hosting a "hanging of the greens" Christmas service and a Passover Seder meal.

The survey yielded additional surprises. I had included several nominal categories on the survey for the sake of comparison. I wanted to be able to contrast possible differences in gender, age, and board perceptions.

A significant difference was found in how younger and older people rated the tradition dimension. Contrary to my expectations, the younger people rated this dimension significantly higher than older generations. Statistically, the people at the most extreme ends of the pool cause any correlation to be significant. And this correlation was significant; the very youngest people in our congregation rated tradition as more important than the very oldest.

I kept asking questions. I initially assumed that maintaining the status quo and preserving tradition were more important for younger people than older people. But after further discussion, it was clear that the younger people were not overly concerned about tradition themselves, but perceiving the older generation to be "traditional," they didn't want to rock the boat. In the end they were happy to hear that another generation in the church was open to change.

This discovery has proved to be both correct and profitable. The congregation has attempted a variety of nontraditional approaches with little or no contention from any segment. This illustration also reveals the extreme importance of using the results of surveys merely as indicators of a church's identity and never as the final word. Whenever you use any survey, check out the results with parishioners before making any change based upon the results.

Several other churches have taken the Survey of Church Distinctiveness and sent me the results. To date, every church that has sent me a copy of its survey results has uncovered a different configuration for the nine dimensions. One church rated evangelism as its most important aspect. Another, benevolence. Another, ministry to members. This kind of reporting is further evidence that the dimensions are truly independent measures of distinctiveness. The survey is doing what it was designed to do. It is revealing how one church differs from all others.

Your Church's Potential

Differences in background, climate, and environment, discussed earlier, lead to great disparities in potential. Comparisons among congregations, in terms of success, are meaningless. A church's mission statement should realistically reflect its own potential. A church's success should be measured against its potential and not someone else's idea of success.

Bobby Knight, Indiana University basketball coach, sometimes gets upset at the most peculiar moments. His team may be ahead by thirty-five points, and he will still lambaste a player for the poor execution of a play. His reasoning is that he evaluates his team against its own potential and, ultimately, against the game of basketball itself, never against the performance of an opponent.

Similarly, churches should evaluate themselves against their own unique opportunities for evangelism, discipleship, and ministry, never against the expectations of a hierarchy or the success of a neighboring church. Judge a program solely on the basis of how much it improved the situation for all involved, and how much it advanced your church's overall mission. But never attempt to make this judgment without first knowing the unique mission for your church.

The Epilogue

As we drove home from a visit to Grandma's house one night, the children watched the houses flick by. Neither child had ever enjoyed traveling; driving somewhere appeared to be a necessary evil to reach a destination. At the ages of five and seven, they no longer protested, but no one would ever convince them that a drive in the country was something that a person would actually choose to do.

This night Kelsey was involved in her usual pastime, wishing we were already home. We had completed about one-fourth of an hour's journey when she remarked, "It looks like we're here on this side."

"Yes," her parents responded in unison, each pondering what she meant but choosing not to spoil the moment by commenting. I remember I interpreted her statement to mean that on one side of the road she saw so many things that looked familiar that she was sure we were almost there. But, upon looking on the other side, she realized that we were not yet in our own neighborhood.

Performing an evaluation procedure within a congregation with only a cursory understanding of that congregation is extremely dangerous. One must look on both sides of the road, so to speak, to truly understand what makes up a congregation.

From a broad perspective, any number of churches may look very similar. Upon closer examination, however, a church may reveal hundreds of idiosyncrasies that set it apart from every other church on the same side of the road. When evaluating anything in a church—a program,

a pastor, a ministry, a staff person—it is essential that the evaluator understand the uniqueness of that congregation. It is impossible to answer
the question of whether a program has advanced a church's *raison d'etre*
if either the church or the evaluator is unclear about where the church is
headed. To detect a church's direction, one must look on both sides of
the road. Failing to do so may lead a church into thinking that it has
arrived, when in reality, it has only begun the journey.

CHAPTER 3

Techniques of Evaluation

There is no one right way to do evaluation. No one evaluation procedure or model will reveal all there is to know about a person's work or a program. This chapter will give a variety of techniques that a reader might employ in formulating evaluation procedures. I present a wide range of techniques because different techniques have different strengths and weaknesses. Some are helpful in evaluating people; others are useful in evaluating programs. Some are better designed to reveal how and when a program works. Others are better at assessing who is affected by a program.

In choosing and designing an evaluation procedure, keep in mind a variety of factors. Different procedures require different resources. Berk and Rossi suggest that "the choice among evaluation methods is conditioned by the resources available and by the amount of precision needed."[1] The choice should also be influenced by what is being evaluated and by who will conduct the evaluation.

Just as there is no one right way to do an evaluation, there is also no reason to avoid evaluation. Avoiding evaluation yourself only means that someone else is going to do it, and that person's motives may not be as compassionate as yours. So, go ahead; take the lead. The one who knows the most is not always asked to take the lead. On the other hand, knowledge is seldom harmful to leaders or followers.

Even though this chapter presents several methods, some of which may sound technical, I still hope you will find this chapter user friendly. I tried to present the methods in a clear, yet concise, way. The methods are arranged from the least complex to the most complex. Ready? Let's go.

Gathering Easy Data

Many evaluation techniques can be employed with very little effort.
Resources, containing lots of useful data, may be no farther away than
your fingertips. If no one in your congregation is familiar with evaluation procedures, it's best to start by exploring existing documents. Even
an expert evaluator should never overlook readily available reports.
Some people immediately want to generate new data for every problem
or issue they attack. Why? I don't know. Guba and Lincoln advise,
"Documents, records, and unobtrusive measures are usually readily
available, and why educational inquirers would not want to use them is
unclear. Records, in particular, are an enormously useful source."[2] For
years investigative journalists have recognized the importance of using
existing documents.[3] Documents can also be a precious resource for
churches.

Most denominations compile annual directories containing information such as worship attendance, Sunday school attendance, gains, losses,
income, and expenses. Why should your church pay attention to this
kind of data? Two main reasons. Data such as these are important in
forming a church's identity and in conducting an evaluation strategy
known as "needs assessment," in which one tries to determine what
types of programs are needed. Identity formation involves building a
picture of who you are as a congregation.

Compiling and tabling this type of information when I came to my
congregation as pastor helped us see that attendance figures had been
declining over the last ten years. This reality did not match the perceptions of the membership. Nearly everyone, when initially asked, had
reported that the church had been extremely stable for a decade. Working with a small group of people to compile the figures proved to be as
meaningful as the product we produced. The small group immediately
took ownership over the data and thoughtfully presented them to the rest
of the congregation.

Ten years is no magic figure. Looking at any number of previous
years can be eye opening. And perceptions often differ from reality.
Reporting actual figures rather than making hunches can compel a
church to look at what is real.

Reporting figures related to attendance and giving can serve many
purposes. A discovered decline may give some church leaders permission

to try something new in terms of outreach or ministry. Some members may say, "Okay, I see now. Maybe we do need to try that program you have been telling us about." It may prompt others to look for and celebrate other aspects of growth not related to attendance, such as growth in maturity, discipleship, ministry, or unity. A discovered increase may help a church understand its need to add a second worship service or another staff person or to commence a building program. No matter what is discovered, examining existing documents eases the congregation into the evaluation process in a nonthreatening manner. It can open the door toward other, more involved, procedures.

Attendance figures are not the only useful information from old church records. Asking a financial expert in the congregation to calculate previous versus current giving (adjusted for inflation) can reveal much about how a church's buying power has been shaped by giving patterns. Calculating the percentage of income that goes toward missions can also be helpful. Some churches keep track of capital expenses as a percentage of income. Why not get copies of your denominational or judicatory directories for the last ten years and turn them over to a group of people who love to play with numbers? The people will be delighted that you asked for their help and will probably discover some very helpful information.

Organizational charts are another good source of information. Turn copies of your organizational structure over to someone who loves to think about "the big picture." Ask for fresh insights into how your church is organized.

Does your church have job descriptions? They, too, are a useful source of information. How often have the job descriptions been altered? Who has input into the alterations? Evaluation can involve an analysis of the descriptions' content and of the way the descriptions are used in your church. Evaluation of procedures is just as important as evaluation of content and can reveal as much about a church's identity as actual documents.

The local courthouse probably contains a storehouse of information for churches. Experts in the field can help the church with demographic studies. Some denominations provide census information as a service to churches. Some will even come and help the church interpret specific census track information. Never be afraid to call on someone else to help. When the data you have obtained are not user friendly, find a human being to help you who is.

Most denominations have personnel available to help churches
analyze a wide range of data. Some provide comprehensive services,
offering to compile requested reports for types of information a church
feels it cannot compile or calculate itself. Ecumenical, parachurch, and
consulting agencies can also help. The Alban Institute has a variety of
personnel gifted in various aspects of evaluation techniques.

Gathering Data with a Little More Effort

With just a little more effort than retrieving on-site documents, but with
less effort than formulating a survey or conducting a set of interviews,
churches can obtain more data from additional sources.

A great deal of information can be gathered by walking through the
neighborhood. Someone has suggested that a part of management
should be done MBWA-style (Management By Walking About). I
believe that a part of church evaluation should be conducted by walking
about. Consider EBWA—Evaluating By Walking About.

Is your church considering an outreach program to neighborhood
youth? Why not evaluate the idea by walking about and counting the
number of toys lying in the front yards of homes close to the church.
Are there more bicycles than toys? Maybe the focus should be teen-
agers. What about basketball hoops? Soccer nets? Swing sets? Shiny
sports cars? This sort of information would also shed light on the possibility of a latch-key program, a day-care program, or a college and career
program.

Is your church considering a weekly Lenten program for business
people? Walk about and discover the predominant business schedule in
your neighborhood. Where do people go to lunch? How long do people
take for lunch?

How is your church perceived by the people close by? Walk around
and find out about some of the people in the neighborhood. They may
have needs that you could never discover by brainstorming in a board
room of the church building.

Evaluation by walking about can reveal information to help set up or
fine-tune a proposed or established program. As the reader can quickly
surmise, an informal analysis of the neighborhood can also help a church
see what types of programs could be dreamed up. Similar to documents

and records, informal observation techniques can be very helpful in needs assessment.

Quantitative Techniques

Quantitative evaluation techniques rely on data that you can categorize and count—through the use of surveys, attitude instruments, personality inventories, and so forth.

Quantitative procedures can be very elaborate or extremely simple. When it comes to quantitative techniques, most organizations rely on surveys. Consider the following list of ten great three-by-five-card surveys. Each reveals something very different about your congregation. You may wish to try one of these next Sunday. Each idea can be processed by passing out an index card to each person present at a meeting or worship event. Ask participants to record their answers to one of the questions below:

1. What are your three favorite hymns?
2. What are the three greatest strengths and weaknesses of this church?
3. What would you like to see our church do next year? Next century?
4. What is your favorite TV show? Current song?
5. Other than today, what is the last worship event you can remember?
6. On what would you like to hear a sermon?
7. How many times did you drive by the church this week?
8. Who first invited you to this church?
9. What are the five things you hold most sacred?
10. List a need that someone might have for which our church could help.

If at all possible, distribute and collect surveys at the same meeting. If you allow people to take surveys home with the intention of returning them, you'll get responses only from people who love to fill out surveys and/or those who have nothing better to do. Those types of respondents could possibly skew your results.

It is much easier and less dangerous to distribute a survey designed by someone else, not yourself. Writing unambiguous questions is hard work. Even experts make mistakes. Remember when findings from a 1992 Roper Survey revealed that 22 percent of Americans believe that the holocaust may never have happened? It turned out that the question contained a double negative. When it was reworded to eliminate the double negative, it was reported that less than 1 percent believe that the holocaust may never have happened.

There are many excellent sources of already validated surveys for churches. Carroll, Dudley, and McKinney's book *Handbook for Congregational Studies* includes surveys for retrieving information related to identity, context, process, and program.[4] Jill Hudson's book *Evaluating Ministry* contains several surveys for a joint evaluation of clergy and congregation.[5]

Sampling

What group are you trying to discover something about? That group is called your population. If you do not choose to give your survey to every member of your population, the smaller group that receives the survey is called a sample of the population group. In most cases, a local church will want to survey its entire population.

Let's say you would like to discover some perceptions from members of your diaconate. If you give your survey to every member of your diaconate, you have surveyed your entire population group.

Let's say you would like to discover some perceptions from your entire church, and you choose to mail a survey to every tenth member, then you have "systematically" sampled your church population. A statistical expert can help you decide when and how to sample a targeted population.

Whether you choose to survey your entire population group or a sample group, there is always a concern if not everyone in your targeted group responds to the survey: Did those people who did not respond differ from those who did? The greater the percentage of people who respond, the less one needs to worry about this concern. But even a few nonrespondents can skew a survey. There are only two ways to know that your survey is not flawed by nonrespondents. The first is to make sure that every person in your target group responds to the survey. The second is to ask a statistician to help you resample your nonrespondents and compare their results with your original respondents.

The most user friendly method of trying to ensure that your survey results indeed match the perceptions of your respondents is to ask them! Check out any results you obtain with the people you are trying to discover something about. After you have compiled the data, take the results back to the group you surveyed and ask, "Do these results seem to make sense to you? Are there any surprises? Were there any questions that you did not understand? What else is there about our group that we already know that confirms or denies these findings?"

Statistical Computations

People dealing with statistics often report results of their data analyses in terms of "the mean." A mean is an average. It is calculated by adding up all of the scores or answers from a particular group and dividing by the number of scores.

A "standard deviation" is a totally separate piece of information from an average and explains the spread of the scores. A low standard deviation would reveal a high degree of consensus among people in a certain group. A high standard deviation would indicate that people in a particular group held diverse opinions.

Many inexpensive calculators will compute both a mean and a standard deviation from the same set of data—at the push of a button. Most calculators with a "stat" button will handle these computations. The Texas Instruments TI-35 sells for about fifteen dollars and will compute a mean and standard deviation. Follow the user friendly directions for entering your data set and amaze your friends with the results.

Computing a mean and standard deviation are two statistics that can help evaluators to begin making sense of the data they have collected. These computations are part of the field known as descriptive statistics. A variety of other computed descriptive statistics can reveal information about a particular data set. One can also compute a host of statistics that "infer" conclusions about the data (inferential statistics). Inferential statistics can be used to try to discover if the perceptions of two groups, such as males and females or laity and pastoral staff, differ from each other. They could be used to see if young people hold perceptions different from an older group.

In computing inferential statistics, you have several options. You could drive to Indiana and audit a statistics class that I teach. You could try to discover if someone in your congregation has this expertise. Or you could pray for divine revelation. (If you were to attempt the third option, I suspect you could find better things to pray for than the ability to compute inferential statistics.) If you enjoy distributing and collecting surveys, the field of statistics is an interesting field to study. You might consider some continuing education in this field. A great deal can be learned about statistics by taking only a few relevant courses.

Qualitative Techniques

Qualitative evaluation techniques gather data that describe the quality of something. It includes observation, interviews, group conversations, focus groups, and ethnographic studies.

Observing

Although evaluation by walking about serves as an observation tool, more formal observation techniques can be employed. Visitors are an excellent source of information because they approach the most traditional aspects of your church life with "fresh eyes." Ask visitors or newer members of your congregation to take notes on a particular aspect of ministry you want to evaluate. The appendix in *The Inviting Church* by Oswald and Leas gives a plan for interviewing visitors to evaluate a congregation's new-member ministry.[6] These observations might be compared with the observations of long-standing members. Some in your congregation will possess greater observation skills than others by virtue of their personality types, careers, and natural abilities.

Interviewing

Interviews serve as an excellent tool for gathering information about a pastor, staff person, or program in the church. Many evaluators choose to identify ten to fifteen key "stakeholders" within an organization and pose similar questions to each of them. Informants should be selected from a cross section of informed people. Pastors, staff, board chairs, heads of task forces or ministries, new members, and old-timers should be chosen, depending on the topics evaluated.

In forming questions, the same care should be taken in qualitative evaluation techniques as in quantitative techniques. Questions often contain a bias, and respondents love to deliver answers they think will make the evaluators happy. It has something to do with our basic human nature.

McIntosh and Rusbuldt's *Planning Growth in Your Church* contains an outstanding set of interview questions about the ministries of evangelism, caring, worship, education, service, and church administration.[7]

Several considerations can aid an evaluator in obtaining good interview data. Individual interviews should run from thirty to sixty minutes in length. Group conversations should run from sixty to ninety minutes. Icebreaking and socializing are important at the beginning of most interviews to help the interviewee relax and establish a rapport with the interviewer. The best way to conduct interviews is to pose questions as they logically arise within the conversation rather than to force them on the interviewee in a preset manner. It's more important that the majority of the questions get asked than that they get asked in a certain order. People conducting individual interviews should practice asking questions, listening for feedback, watching for nonverbal cues, recording responses, and establishing rapport—all of which will help gain better information.

Video- or audio-taping interviews may make individual respondents nervous; always gain permission before recording. Some interviewers ask a friend or colleague to help "debrief" them immediately following an interview, and some even videotape these sessions. (The time immediately following the interview will yield the best recall of information.) Interviewers may choose to interview groups as well as individual people. Taping group interviews or conversations is usually perceived to be less intimidating. Still, do not tape without the knowledge of the interviewees. Once a group conversation has begun, the members will seem to get lost in one another and quickly become oblivious to observers or recording devices. A good group interviewer will fade into the group as well.

Conducting Focus Groups

Some evaluators have attempted to use focus groups to gather information. This technique is easily misunderstood and often mishandled in a local church situation. Here's the theory behind this method: Gather people together who have much in common but have never met one another; encourage them to have a conversation about a particular topic. The commonality in the group encourages conversation. The anonymity promotes a sense of confidentiality within the group. Each member feels *I will probably never see this person again anyway, so why not say what I really feel this time?* In a local church setting, a focus-group organizer can no doubt achieve commonality in terms of cultures, backgrounds, and socio-economic status. But anonymity is nearly impossible within one local church. Conducting a focus group requires special skills and training.

Using Quantitative and Qualitative Techniques in One Evaluation Procedure

Both quantitative and qualitative techniques can serve well in various types of congregational evaluation, including staff, laity, and program evaluation. Using both types of procedures can give you complementary results. Qualitative techniques more effectively discern side effects and the overall impact of a person or program. Quantitative techniques better reveal how the entire church or a subgroup perceives a particular set of previously defined issues; they also help to show how two or more subgroups differ with respect to particular issues.

Qualitative techniques are often used at the beginning stages of an evaluation procedure to identify the issues. The evaluation team may then employ quantitative techniques to survey an entire group or church about those issues.

Epilogue

Walking into my house the other day, I was greeted: "You'll never believe what I caught your son doing today." Such a statement is truly a greeting. It often reveals much about the state of mind of the speaker and presents great expectations for a response from the one being greeted. What more could you ask for in a greeting?

This particular time, though, the tone did not match the potentially judgmental words. There was a curious smile on my wife's face. She had observed my son making marks on a piece of paper after every subsequent rolling of a particular toy car. She asked him what he was doing.

"I noticed that there was something wrong with this car," he replied. "When I roll it, sometimes it lands on its side, sometimes right side up, and sometimes upside down. I decided to keep track of how it landed each time, so I could tell what kind of car I had."

After the story, my wife offered her commentary, "He is your son, and it's scary."

There are probably people in your congregation who truly enjoy working with numbers and statistics. While you may find this phenomenon strange, even disturbing, take advantage of the reality. Asking certain people to help you analyze data will be like giving those people a gift. At the same time, employ a few less-erudite types to keep your evaluation procedures balanced.

CHAPTER 4

A Fill-in-the-Blanks Evaluation

This chapter will help you begin to apply some evaluation principles to your local setting. Before you read any further in this chapter, close the book and think of a program in your church that you would like to evaluate. Got it? So do I. I have chosen an evangelism program known as Friend Day. Now, we can proceed.

I will pose ten questions that could be asked of any program you might have chosen. The questions may be posed in any order. They are:

1. What is the background of the program?
2. What is the philosophy of the program?
3. What are the biases?
4. Who are the stakeholders?
5. How can we create a relaxed atmosphere throughout the evaluation?
6. What is the merit and worth of the program?
7. What are the tradeoffs for being involved in the program?
8. Is the program advancing the unique character of our church?
9. What side effects have occurred?
10. How can we improve the program?

What is the background of the program?

Discovering the background of any program can be extremely important. Without inquiring into the background of the program, a church will often choose a program because someone suggested it, it sounded exciting in an article, or another church tried it. But it is wise to inquire about a program's background before the program is chosen. Even if a program has already been implemented, it is never too late to analyze the background as part of the evaluation.

Several types of questions can be asked about the background of a program. Who designed the program? Was it laity, clergy, researchers, a parachurch organization, an ecumenical organization, or a denominational staff person? Which denomination? Was it tested anywhere else? What were the results? How many have tried it? Who was its original target audience? Can you talk to anyone who has actually implemented it? The answers to these questions can help a church decide whether a program is right for it or why certain aspects of a program produced positive results while others did not.

When our church implemented a Friend Day program, we recognized that this model had been marketed by different sources, and we went with a version that had already been altered with our denomination in mind. We read the success stories of other churches and noted the size of their churches and the results.

What is the philosophy of the program?

We strongly agreed with the philosophy of the chosen Friend Day program, listed as, "Hospitality and a friendly welcome for guests as well as worship and a sermon which clearly communicates friendship with Jesus Christ are the focus of Friend Day Sunday."[1]

Most churches could embrace the philosophy of such a Friend Day program. But other programs may not suit as many settings. Sometimes churches try to implement programs that do not coincide with their overall mission and identity. I recently heard a pastor comment on a church growth program that had been designed and sponsored by one specific congregation.

He lamented, "Several members of our congregation attended the training sessions for the program. We came home and began to implement the program to the letter. It took us six months to realize that we just were not like the church that founded this program. On the outside we were trying to be like that other church, but on the inside, we were still a very different congregation."

What are the biases?

Every evaluator has a particular set of notions about the program or person being evaluated. It is helpful if the evaluator, rather than pretending to be unbiased, lists a set of personal assumptions or biases from the inception of any program or its evaluation. Defining one's views will benefit all·involved, including anyone who may read the evaluation report. The evaluator might ask these questions: What are my particular views about this program, person, or ministry before I begin? What are my assumptions about issues related to this program? Should I test out any of my assumptions prior to beginning the evaluation? How am I likely to view this particular program differently from my colleagues? How would I choose to define the terms and concepts that I will deal with in the evaluation? How do I view this program in relation to the life of our congregation? What is its relative weight? Considering one's answers to these types of questions can add credibility to the evaluation process.

In evaluating our Friend Day program, I had to admit that I was biased in favor of the program. I had long since bought into the concept of friendship evangelism or relational evangelism. So I had to be very careful to look for sincere ways in which the program might be improved and be extra alert to negative opinions, opinions I would be incapable of registering if I did not know my biases prior to the evaluation.

Who are the stakeholders?

The stakeholders of a program are the people who have a vested interest in the program. "Stakeholders include policymakers; the ones who administer the program; the persons who deliver the services; and the beneficiaries of the program."[2]

Defining the stakeholders helps you know whom to initially interview or survey and who should have the most influence regarding the future of the program. Not all opinions should be weighted equally. The opinions of key stakeholders should be weighted more than the opinions of others. After all, they are the ones who have most "at stake" in the program.

A stakeholder does not necessarily favor either the program itself or the results of the evaluation. "In almost all program issues, stakeholders may be aligned on opposing sides, some favoring the program and some opposing. Whatever the outcome of the evaluation, usually some are pleased and some are disappointed. It is impossible to please everyone."[3]

Stakeholders in the Friend Day program included visitors who attended on Friend Day Sunday, the task force that designed the program, the evangelism ministry team, and the people most affected by changes in logistics on any particular Sunday.

Several changes were made to accommodate the Friend Day visitors, changes that might have negatively affected some of the "regulars." While the proponents of the Friend Day program suggested offering a "normal Sunday" for visitors to experience, the increased number of total worshippers warranted some changes in procedures. For example, four topical Sunday school adult classes were scheduled. It was feared that visitors would not attend the "regular" classes; if they did, space would be a problem. Also, regular members were asked to carpool and to leave parking spaces near the entrances open for visitors. A part of the evaluation assessed attitudes of the regulars about the changes made on Friend Day. Their responses alerted us to procedures that could be performed more effectively the next time the program is implemented—and to changes that could be made every Sunday to accommodate visitors with little disturbance to the regulars.

How can we create a relaxed atmosphere throughout the evaluation?

There are several problems in trying to obtain *honest* responses from people. This "truth" issue doesn't mean that the respondents are not Christian. It just means that they are human. People have a need for, and enjoy, praise. This reality serves as a motivation to help others. Whenever an evaluator asks someone a question, that person will usually be motivated to give the evaluator a pleasing answer. That is not necessarily what is desired. To continually improve a program, evaluators need honest responses.

The penchant for the positive is not the only obstacle in receiving candid answers. Sometimes respondents will give answers clouded by their defensiveness or their investment in the program. Still others "freeze up" when they know their answers are being taped, recorded, or, at the very least, used as a basis for future decision making.

You can enhance more honest responses by creating a relaxed atmosphere for the respondent. Several ideas can help create a relaxed atmosphere. Always assure the respondent of the confidentiality of his answers. When beginning an interview, allow the respondent some time to get acquainted with the interviewer. Always let the respondents know exactly how you intend to use the information you receive. Be prepared to answer these questions: Why are you obtaining the information? Who will read the results?

When we interviewed visitors who had attended our Friend Day service, we stated the reason for the interview: to try to discover how the program was perceived by them and how it could be improved if we decided to try it again the following year. We conducted a few very short interviews with people chosen at random. When interviewing people who are not members of your congregation, you should not ask for much of their time. Members, on the other hand, will often give as much time as you deem necessary.

What is the merit and worth of the program?

Many evaluations address and assess the value of a program. But value in what sense? There are two possibilities.

> It may have value of its own, implicit, inherent, independent of any possible applications. *Merit* describes this kind of intrinsic, context-free value. . . . On the other hand, an entity may have value within some context of use or application. *Worth* describes this kind of extrinsic or context-determined value.[4]

One can quickly recognize both the merit and worth of a Friend Day program. A program of this nature has merit in its potential for introducing someone to Christ. In any church, this act is part of the Great Commission and thus has great merit.

The program also has potential worth to our local congregation. After reading the reported results of other churches, we discovered that many churches had increased their average Sunday morning worship attendance following the implementation of the program. Our church viewed this possibility as a positive. This same concept, however, may or may not have worth for every congregation. Believe it or not, not all churches want to grow numerically. Growing numerically causes drastic changes in a church, and some churches, not having come to grips with the potential problems that growth can cause, unconsciously sabotage evangelism programs. For pastors, increased numbers mean increased responsibility, increased work, sharing ministry, having members one cannot pastor, and revising theology.[5] For the laity, growth means increased giving, readjusting fellowship groups, and opening up the leadership circles.[6]

Our church has previously discussed the changes that numerical growth can cause and has made a conscious decision to attempt programs aimed at growing numerically, hoping that the advantages of growth will outweigh the potential adjustments required by the growth.

What are the tradeoffs for being involved in the program?

There are only so many people available to perform the ministries of a congregation. The number of hours poured into one ministry will not be available to pour into another ministry. People cannot be two places at one time. Being involved in one ministry always means not being involved in another.

After implementing the Friend Day program for several years, we found it helpful to involve new members in the Friend Day task force planning group. New members can sing the successes of the program, often because they were first introduced to our church on a previous Friend Day Sunday. They provide fresh insights into possible ways to enhance the program. But there are only so many new members each year. Involving them in this program means that we probably cannot involve them in anything else too soon, lest a new member become burned out by being too involved too quickly.

Likewise, there are only so many resources available for programming. Friend Day is a very inexpensive program to implement, so this was not a great concern in this case. But at other times, our church has had to plan more than one year in advance to implement a major program requiring several leaders and several dollars.

When evaluating a program, ask, "If our church were not involved in this program, what other program could we be involved in?" Is it worth the tradeoff? Never continue a program solely on the basis of tradition.

Is the program advancing the unique character of our church?

My church's style of evangelism works to add new members to the congregation and to assimilate each new person into the church family. We were initially concerned about the Friend Day program in light of our evangelism strategy. Would we add too many members too quickly and not be able to assimilate them? But in actuality from the Friend Day program we saw another pattern emerge: People joined the church after varying degrees of involvement and attendance. A few people joined very quickly, while others needed to get to know us better over a longer period of time. I recall one couple that eventually joined; their first two visits were on two successive Friend Days a year apart!

What side effects have occurred?

In evaluating a program, try to discover a much broader range of outcomes than merely, "Did the program accomplish what it was intended to accomplish?" Some programs may indeed accomplish their intended goals but cause so many other problems that it would not be beneficial ever to implement the program again. Other programs may not meet their intended aims, but many other positive side effects warrant keeping the program. In discovering negative side effects, evaluators seldom have to travel very far. People are usually vocal about disturbing effects from a new program. But it may be necessary to expand the list of respondents beyond the initial list of stakeholders to discover the positive side effects of a program.

Our Friend Day program produced very few negative, but several positive, side effects. The inviting atmosphere of the Friend Day program permeated other aspects of our church. We had often talked of trying to become a more welcoming congregation throughout the year.

The preevent emphasis and training for Friend Day and postevent follow-up proved to be a catalyst for promoting ourselves as a welcoming congregation year-round. We added several new permanent signs pointing to the nursery, rest rooms, and Sunday school classes. Parking patterns were adjusted permanently to welcome visitors. A permanent welcoming ministry was added to enhance the work of the Sunday morning greeters. The positive side effects from this program were numerous.

How can we improve the program?

There are two main types of evaluation. The first, summative evaluation, asks whether or not this program should be continued. The second, formative evaluation, seeks constantly to improve a program. Implementers of a program should adopt an evaluator's mind set all the way through a program's adoption and implementation. Too often evaluators begin to evaluate only after the completion of a program.

Every time our Friend Day task force met, evaluative questions were asked. Have you heard any complaints or praises about this program yet? Should we adjust this particular aspect of the program? Is there a better way? Then, once a program has run its course, formative evaluation procedures should be employed along with summative evaluation procedures. Summative evaluation merely helps decide whether the program should be chosen again for implementation. If the decision is yes, formative evaluation provides all of the information for how to improve the program next time around. Formative and summative evaluation are complementary parts of a comprehensive evaluation strategy.

Epilogue

I was driving my daughter, Kelsey, home from an outing when she posed one of her curiosities.

"Daddy, when is Cathy [her aunt] going to get a baby?"

"Well," I responded, "people usually wait until they get married to have a baby."

"Oh" was followed by several seconds of silence while the wheels turned on both the car and my daughter's brain. Finally, she continued,

"She hasn't found a man she really likes?"

"I guess not," I replied. Then I asked, "What qualities would you like to find in a husband, Kelsey?"

"What's qualities?"

I thought it best to give examples rather than try to describe the abstract term I had just introduced. "Would you like your husband to be funny? Nice to you? Able to talk about things you like to talk about?"

Again, following a long pause, she said in her most disgusted tone, "Daddy, that's you."

I suppose she wanted help in differentiating among men she might choose as her husband, and I hadn't given her any help. Of course I would like for her to choose a husband just like me. And, if making the choice today, she might choose someone very similar, although I am certain that will change rapidly.

When people make evaluations, they often have trouble viewing a situation through an unbiased lens. In fact, it is probably ridiculous to think that an unbiased evaluation is ever performed. Better to be honest about our biases and compare the results of any evaluation in light of our biases. What is it you would like to see most? Remember that when you evaluate.

CHAPTER 5

Evaluation and Church Renewal

During the 1990s church renewal has become to churches what love is to soap operas. It is quite possibly the most talked about and least understood topic among churches today.

I believe that one of the reasons for the confusion about church renewal is the lack of a clear working definition of *church renewal.* In this chapter I will present a comprehensive definition of church renewal. The definition by no means signals the end of discussion on the church renewal matter. Rather, it is intended as a springboard for intelligent dialogue. Before one can evaluate an issue, one must know something about that issue. So before one can evaluate church renewal, one must know something about church renewal. Following a presentation of my church renewal model, I will conclude the chapter by presenting a survey for diagnosing the renewal strategy you may currently be using.

If you wish to evaluate a specific renewal program in your church, use the evaluation tools described in chapters 3 and 4. Chapter 5 will help you evaluate your comprehensive renewal strategy.

A Definition of Church Renewal

Church renewal is not merely individual spiritual renewal performed on a grand scale! It is a renewal of the body of Christ. The body of Christ shows its most visible expression in the form of a local church, which contains a personality, identity, life, history, and future all its own. So church renewal is a renewal of the whole congregation—the entire local church. Upon this basis, I present my definition of church renewal:

Church renewal occurs when a distinct group of people expect the Spirit of God to challenge, direct, and empower them to reach their potential of being the church in today's world.

Daily Church Renewal

Carefully constructed within this definition are several assumptions about the renewal process. Let me explain.

First, renewal is a continual process. The goal of churches should be to become renewing churches rather than renewed churches. Individual Christians have, for the most part, accepted and enthusiastically embraced the need for continual renewal. Romans 12:2 says, "Do not be conformed to this world, but be transformed by the renewing of your minds. . . ." Christians tacitly accept the fact that God calls them into daily renewal. The recent emphasis upon daily devotions, personal retreats, and covenant groups speaks to the wide acceptance of a daily renewal model for Christians.

Not nearly as accepted, however, is an emphasis on continual renewal for local congregations. Resources abound that emphasize steps and conditions for church renewal. Follow these ten steps to renewal. Meet these seven conditions and you will have achieved church renewal. McIntosh and Rusbuldt[1] and Fothergill[2] present a finite number of renewal steps. Snyder,[3] Schaller,[4] and Buttry[5] talk of conditions. What happens once the steps or conditions have been completed? Does the church start the process all over again? Do they embrace another set of steps from a new author or proponent of church renewal?

Most programs within a church have the ability to incite renewal. But eventually a church needs to ask how all of those programs are working together to bring daily, substantive renewal to a congregation. Churches should consider a formative evaluation of their ongoing renewal efforts. For too long, the church has been in a problem-solving mode. They think about renewal only when something appears to be wrong. Maxam conducted a church renewal research project operating from a premise that identified church renewal proponents as "individuals or groups who are implicitly or explicitly critical of the contemporary life, thought, or practice of the Christian Church and who seek to work independently and corporately to change the church."[6] The assumptions behind Maxam's definition are still held by many people today: People turn toward church renewal only when they perceive something to be drastically wrong with their church. It is time to let go of that assumption and embrace a daily emphasis on church renewal.

The Spirit Renews the Church

I hold a second assumption about church renewal: that the church does not renew itself. The Holy Spirit challenges, directs, and empowers the work of renewal. "It takes more than clever social engineering to bring about renewal."[7] The Spirit of God renews the church. Many church renewal resources coerce the pastoral leadership into feeling responsible for the church's state of renewal. That's simply not biblical. Pastoral leadership has a great deal to do with the activities in the congregation, but renewal results are the sole property of God's handiwork. Even Paul, who liked to tell churches that he had more to boast about than anyone else if he chose to do so, reminded the church, "I planted, Apollos watered, but God gave the growth" (1 Cor. 3:6). God is the one who provides growth and renewal for churches. Numerical growth. Common-bond growth. Growth in maturity. All kinds of growth. God is the source.

Continuous Updating

My church renewal definition is built on a third assumption, that renewal involves updating. Church renewal involves ministering in *today's* world. In my pretentious seminary days, I once embarked on a class project attempting to discover the most historically accurate form of church structure present in churches today. I quickly discovered that New Testament churches used a variety of structures to achieve their strategies. There is no one right way to organize, plan, elect officers, or carry out the ministries of God.

As the needs of people change, so must the practices of the church. The goal is to present the good news—the same good news presented centuries ago—to people of our day. This means adopting new forms and procedures. It also means meeting needs that may not have existed before. Jesus never encouraged an AIDS ministry, a latch-key program, counseling for families victimized by drunk drivers, or a ministry to people recovering from gambling addictions. Had those needs existed in Jesus' day, he probably would have addressed them in some way. Renewal entails updating. Updating structures, ministries, procedures, and strategies. The message of the gospel has not changed, but everything else has.

Reaching Your Renewal Potential

A final assumption foundational to my church renewal definition is that the potential for renewal in every congregation will be dramatically different from any other church. The only yardstick to which a church should measure its renewal efforts is its own potential. In an earlier chapter I encouraged churches never to compare themselves to other churches in terms of accomplishments. This applies especially to the area of church renewal.

Comparing your church's renewal efforts with another church's usually leads to comparing numbers, and the evaluation of renewal efforts are better served by qualitative than quantitative techniques. Renewal is never a matter of mere numbers. Just as an individual can sense when she is being spiritually renewed, so can a church intuitively discern when it has become a renewing church, all the while recognizing that this achieved status may change at any moment.

In terms of goals for renewal, a congregation should aspire for increasingly more of its activities to become renewing activities. "Renewing churches" not "renewed churches." A church can never ensure that an activity will lead to renewal because God is the one responsible for renewal, not the church. But a constant, formative evaluation of one's renewal efforts will help a church discover which activities in the past have been more renewing than others, and which activities in the future might lead to a greater sense of daily congregational renewal.

Is your church currently in the state of being a renewing congregation? How do your members feel after gathering for worship? What happens when boards get together? What has been the primary focus for task forces in the past year? Is your church constantly striving to meet brand new needs in your community? Are the organizational structures and procedures within your congregation readily adaptable to new opportunities? The answers to these questions will help a church decide whether or not it has become a renewing congregation. If you're not there yet, read on for help in becoming a renewing church.

Avenues to Renewal

Now that we have a working definition of church renewal, let me introduce a concept for carrying out renewal in a local church. In the next several pages, I invite you to consider the concept of *avenues to church renewal*. An avenue to renewal is a pathway for allowing the Spirit of God to renew the church. I believe that at least three such avenues exist in every congregation: the avenues of awakening, reformation, and mission.

Awakening Avenue

The awakening avenue to renewal incorporates all of the means and strategies a church employs to experience the presence of God. Every church has some concept of how it approaches God and how it receives direction from God. The "destination" or goal of this avenue is a church experiencing as much of the presence of God as possible. Strategies aimed at improving the link between a church and God are renewal strategies.

The following activities would fall into the awakening avenue: spirituality retreats, worship planning groups, covenant prayer groups,[8] cell groups, liturgical models of worship, praise models of worship, music ministries, Renovare,[9] *lectio divina*,[10] Kerygma, and Emmaus Walk Weekends.[11] A church desiring to emphasize the awakening avenue might consider one of those events.

Reformation Avenue

The reformation avenue to renewal incorporates all a church's plans, hopes, dreams, visions, and pictures of the future. This is the avenue that updates and envisions. A church that wishes to emphasize this avenue would begin by asking how church structures could be improved to enable more renewal. Considering new models of ministry, designing new worship services, rethinking the board structure, holding envisioning and planning retreats, and redesigning the constitution—all are reformation activities.

The reformation avenue is probably the most difficult to conceptualize as renewal activity. But think in these terms: Often a church will wonder why a number of launched programs aimed at renewal have never achieved that goal. Through evaluation, it might discover that it has been pouring new ideas into old, outdated wineskins. Once a church has burst its wineskins enough times, it realizes that reformation can be just as much a part of renewal as awakening and mission. The churches that practice reformation and envisioning are not preparing for future renewal; they are doing renewal now.

Mission Avenue

The third avenue of church renewal, mission, is what most people think of when they think of renewal activities. It is the ministry branch of renewal. I believe that a part of every Christian's growth is blocked until that person gets involved in a ministry. It is the same with the church. Ministries in the church spark renewal.

The potential for church-based ministries are endless because new needs arise perpetually. Most recently, our church has become involved in Habitat for Humanity and a twelve-step support group. We have held community seminars in stress management and financial planning training. Other churches in our community have offered a day out for mothers and caregivers. Several churches in Chicago commenced a parish nurse program for people who needed to talk to someone about a problem that was both spiritual and physical.[12]

Churches become renewing churches by regularly reporting their ministry involvements. Ask people to deliver ministry testimonies during worship. Consider the budget of your church a mission budget. Write up and send in the ministries of your church to one of your denominational papers. Help people discover their spiritual gifts and opportunities to use them. Ministry activities are renewing activities.

More about Avenues to Renewal

The three avenues just described form the basis for renewal in many congregations. The names of these three avenues are not sacred. If you discover a more operationally helpful term, use it. You may also discover other avenues to renewal in your specific situation.

Understanding the concept of avenues to renewal is perhaps more crucial to an understanding of your church's renewal strategy than embracing the three specific avenues just described. To ensure that the concept of avenues to renewal is not misunderstood, let me give a little more explanation of what I mean by the phrase.

An avenue to renewal is something that already exists in a church. It is not a program, a resource, or a book that a church may purchase. Every church already possesses some means of renewal. I've never met a church member who could not articulate some means through which his church had experienced renewal in both the past and present. Pathways to renewal are already present in your congregation.

All avenues to renewal in your congregation are fluid—constantly changing—not static. Your church's understanding and design of a-wakening to God will change each time you gather for worship. Your church's idea of reformation and its vision of the future will reshape after each article and book read by the leadership and each new experience of the membership. Your church's mission avenue will readjust as the merits and worth of each new program are debated.

Avenues to renewal run parallel to one another. Unlike steps or strategies to renewal, no order is implied by the order in which the avenues have been presented. At any one point in time, churches are usually emphasizing one avenue over the others. At different points throughout the history of your congregation, you have probably placed primary emphasis on each of the three avenues.

But emphasizing one avenue over another does not make the other avenues disappear. The avenues maintain an interdependent nature. Activity in one avenue will influence the fluid nature of the other two avenues. Often renewing activity in one avenue will enhance the potential of the other avenues. For example, as a church adjusts its worship to open it up more to the Spirit of God, that presence of the Spirit will probably lead to changes in its reformation and mission avenues. An individual seldom hears the call of God to stay put. Likewise, for a church.

As it hears the call of God more clearly, it will be able to mold its vision more explicitly and live out its call more intentionally.

Evaluating the Avenues to Renewal

Which avenue should your church currently be emphasizing the most? The answer will probably depend on which avenue is providing the most renewing triumphs for your church. Which avenue, do you suppose, is the strongest and which avenue is the weakest in your congregation? I have devised a survey for discovering just that. The survey is designed to help your church discover which of the three avenues of awakening, reformation, and mission is currently the strongest and weakest in your congregation. You can find the survey in appendix B, "Church Renewal Diagnosis Instrument." (You have permission to photocopy the survey.) It may be administered to one small group, several small groups, or the entire congregation. Answers from different groups may be compared or pooled together. Keep in mind the chapter 3 tips for administering surveys.

Once the results are discovered, take time to test out the results with those who took the survey and the rest of your congregation. Remember that the results of a survey are merely indicative and never conclusive. Depending on the discrepancies among the three avenues, you may wish to capitalize on the current strongest avenue or to build up the weakest. Once again, survey knowledge is useful only when incorporated with other knowledge that you already have about your congregation.

Epilogue

One year I asked my daughter what she would like for Christmas.

"I'd like to be bigger than my brother," she replied. She apparently wanted to be bigger or older. Either would have satisfied her.

I tried to explain to her how difficult a request she had made. There may come a time when she might be taller, given the maturity rates of boys and girls, but the age thing is a little harder. Perhaps, when she is 100 and her brother forgets that he is 102, she might be able to convince her brother that she has become older. But all she would have changed is perception and not reality. That may be enough.

Certain things in life we must live with. For others, we can at least alter our perception of them. A church will always be burdened or enhanced, as the case may be, by its past.

Some congregations dream of being like other congregations. Pastors dream of being like other pastors. No congregation or pastor can steal someone else's future. Every congregation can, however, experience renewal. Renewal every day. For many congregations, desiring daily renewal would involve a dramatic change in mind set. Many churches have never thought about the possibility of seeking daily renewal. If they did, that change in perception would mean more to them than any potential change in their circumstances. Churches need to long for the Spirit of God more than they long to be like another church.

CHAPTER 6

Evaluation and Lay Ministry

Up to this point, I have focused on evaluation in broad categories. I have presented tools for evaluating and assessing programs, identities, and strategies for renewal. In the next two chapters, I rotate the spotlight toward people. This chapter provides a framework for evaluating the work of laity. The following chapter will discuss evaluation of pastors and pastoral staff.

This chapter will primarily deal with evaluating the laity's ministry. Several of the evaluation tools mentioned in chapter 3 could be employed to evaluate other aspects of laity development and involvement, possibly the devotional practices, prayer patterns, giving trends, or learning skills of laity. In this chapter I present one primary tool for evaluating the ministry of the laity; I encourage laity to ask evaluative questions regarding their ministry roles within the various environments in which they function.

Who Are the Laity?

I believe that every Christian is called to minister. Ordained and non-ordained people are ministry partners in a local congregation. Ministry is part of maturing as a Christian, along with personal spiritual growth, development in witnessing, growth in giving, and discipleship. All people called by God to become Christians are also called to minister. Ministering to others is not optional for anyone in the church.

Having held this hypothesis so forcefully for so long, I can hardly believe I'm writing a book chapter with the word *laity* in the title. I believe the term as generally understood is no longer consistent with partner-oriented ministry. Hans-Reudi Weber writes, "The term 'laity' has always been problematic, and I believe that we have come to a dead end with this designation."[1]

Maria Harris states, "The central question this presents is whether one can take the word 'minister' and preface it with the term 'lay' without at the same time placing the lay minister in a subordinate position."[2]

"No matter how it is interpreted," George Peck adds, "the word 'lay' implies less than positive judgment."[3]

We continue using the term, however, because there is currently no alternative. Although a great number of people have expressed their dissatisfaction with the term *laity*, no one has yet suggested a replacement term. So I keep on using the term, and apologizing for it. Some writers have made great strides using inclusive language. Surely someone will soon similarly develop more equivalent language for laity and clergy.

While I am upset by any term that implies that one Christian's ministry is more important than another's, I react positively to distinctions that exist between clergy and laity. Real-life contrasts between clergy and laity led me to present the evaluation tools for these two groups in two separate chapters in this book. Clergy should be evaluated differently from laity for several reasons. Clergy and laity often integrate ministry and theology in different ways.

> The preacher starts with the theology and then works it into examples of real-life situations. The layperson starts with the real-life situation and then has a need for the theology which applies to it. The difference is crucial.[4]

Both laity and clergy minister within the community and the church. Both groups often carry out similar ministries within the community, serving on task forces and boards alongside one another. Within the domain of the church, however, the two groups minister in differing ways. Within the church, the primary cleric role is to train and equip the laity to minister to one another. Laity also have an entire arena for ministry not possessed by clergy. Unless a pastor is bivocational, the laity will have a workplace ministry that the clergy do not have. Ministry in the workplace can be carried out only by people in the workplace.

The ministries of clergy and laity are indeed different. Different but not hierarchical. No one's ministry is less important than anyone else's ministry.

Where Do Laity Minister?

Now that we have taken a look at who the laity are, let us consider more closely the milieu of their ministry. One of the hardest aspects of any evaluation process is knowing what to evaluate. More church leaders and followers would probably perform more evaluations of a comprehensive nature if they knew where to begin. In previous chapters I have attempted to provide some basic tools for conducting evaluations and a floor plan that could be modified by the evaluator. Here I will again propose a starting point for conducting an evaluation of the ministry of the laity. I believe that there are three primary arenas for the ministry of the laity: the church, the community, and the workplace. Let us begin with the arena evaluated least often, the workplace.

Evaluating Lay Ministry in the Workplace

For too long too much distance has been placed between the workplace and the church. Laypeople talk of not being able to connect what happens on Sunday with what happens on Monday. It's a different world outside of the church walls than it used to be. My wife recently made the decision to reenter the work force after our children started school. As I listen to suspenseful stories involving retailers, co-workers, and colleagues in her field, I realize how different the lives of some of the people in the community are compared to the lives of people with whom I regularly interact as a pastor.

The church has often failed in its aid to laity ministering in the workplace. Celia Hahn explains,

> It is easy to understand why the church would tend to emphasize those needs it can meet, to appear to claim a patent on religion, while ignoring whatever is outside its control: personal religion and the life of the laity in the world.[5]

Hahn, in her book *Lay Voices in an Open Church*, also notes that people in a congregation often do not even know where fellow members work, let alone the workplace ministries they are performing. "I expect to know about fellow parishioners' family situations, divorces, and difficulties with children," she states, "but our lives as workers do not seem to be the lives we share in church."[6]

Prophet, Priest, and King

As a way of relating biblical calls and challenges to the workplace, William Broholm has suggested assessing lay ministry in terms of the typology of prophet, priest, and king.[7]

Functions such as teaching, critiquing, and envisioning are included in one's prophetic ministry. Not everyone can perform those tasks on the job, but for those who do, the Bible has something to say about prophetic performance.

Other workers may view their work as relating more to the priestly function of ministry, which involves modeling, caring, and celebrating.

Finally, kingly ministry is lived out by marketing and distributing, managing, and building. A layperson may identify closely with only one of these categories of ministry or a combination of the three. Insight into how to evaluate one's roles in the workplace may be gained by studying passages of scripture related to functions of prophet, priest, and king.

This typology provides an initial framework for formulating evaluative questions about one's workplace ministry.

Prophetic Questioning

One who is naturally involved in teaching may ask, "How prophetic is my ministry? How can I teach in a way that will benefit my students for a very long time? Are my critiquing skills beneficial, or do they merely come across as judgmental?"

Priestly Questioning

A nurse, doctor, or other person involved in a service industry may
readily identify with the priestly function of ministry and begin formulating questions to help evaluate workplace ministry. One might ask,
"Do I have the interests of the whole person in mind? Am I setting a
good example for my colleagues who are caring for the same people as
I? Do I find time to celebrate with people who have a reason to celebrate? Do I find time to provide a ministry of presence with people
who are in need? Have I discovered meaningful ways to help others
grieve?" Someone once suggested that ritual provides an effective win-
dow allowing a person to pass from one season of life to another. Laity
involved in helping others might ask if they are providing the necessary
opportunities for the ones they serve to pass from one stage of life to
another.

Kingly Questioning

People involved in managing may ask questions of stewardship in evaluating their efforts. Pharaoh once told Joseph, "You shall be over my
house, and all my people shall order themselves as you command; only
with regard to the throne will I be greater than you. . . . See, I have set
you over all the land of Egypt" (Gen. 41:40–41). Pharaoh made Joseph
his chief steward. We, as Christians, are God's stewards. God has given
us responsibility to care for what has been created. We are to care for
the earth and its resources just as God would care for it.
    Likewise, workplace managers are to care for the items within their
jurisdiction just as the owner would care for them. In fact, the steward is
instructed to leave the items in better shape than when they were given to
the steward. In the parable of the talents, the individual given one talent
is not punished for losing the talent but, rather, for remaining idle with
the resources given. Managers are to manage resources in such a way
that improves them. They are to market, distribute, manage, and build
with great wisdom. This is the ministry of stewardship. It is the ideal
standard of ministry in the workplace for the Christian manager.
    Broholm's terms may be helpful for someone who feels as if her
ministry is far removed from the traditional functions of ministry and

would like workplace activities to be considered more closely in line with biblical ministry functions. Laity might find comfort in viewing their on-the-job activities as related to those of prophet, priest, or king. Others may not find this typology as beneficial and choose to evaluate their workplace ministry in another way.

Job Descriptions

Carolyn MacDougall suggests a different typology that can be helpful in assessing lay ministry.[8] She bases her questions for lay ministry evaluation on the job description of the person in the workplace. She suggests that a Christian in the workplace ask evaluative questions in the following three areas: (1) What tasks within my job description can be viewed as ministry tasks? (2) How can I move beyond my job description to perform ministries? (3) When does my job description come into conflict with my values as a Christian?

Doing Ministry by Doing One's Job

Tasks such as serving others, empowering others, and working as a team are part of some people's job descriptions. Christians can have a meaningful ministry simply by performing those aspects of their job description to the best of their ability. Looking at these work aspects is the first level of analysis. At this first level, a layperson should ask, "How can I have a ministry in my workplace by performing well certain aspects of my job description?" Some Christians may find that much of their job description is consistent with ministry-oriented tasks. Others may find that very little, or even absolutely nothing, in their job description could be defined as ministry related.

Going beyond the Job Description

Regardless of how much of one's job description is ministry related, Christians can consider going beyond their job descriptions in maintaining a workplace ministry. A retail person might ask, "How responsive

have I been to my customers in their needs?" A professional might ask,
"How can I integrate a display of the gifts of God's Spirit with my own
abilities?" A manager might ask, "How can I show concern for the
whole person?" A factory worker might ask, "What do my actions reveal about my relationship to God?" Any worker might ask, "If the
people in this workplace had no other contact with any other Christian,
what kind of impression would they have of God, based upon my behavior?" Paul told the Corinthian Christians that they would be the only
letter from God read by some people (2 Cor. 3:2). When Jesus delivered
the Sermon on the Mount, he challenged followers to go beyond what is
expected. He talked of turning the other cheek, carrying a soldier's
backpack an extra mile, and giving to everyone who begs of them (Matt.
5:38-42).

Challenging a Defined Role

For some workers, job descriptions will come into direct conflict with
Christian values. At times the team or unit or division one works with
will make a decision inconsistent with one's values. What gifts should
buyers for businesses accept? Does the mere acceptance of a gift imply
future favoritism? Are the sales tactics of the firm in line with the sales-
person's personal values? Recognition of conflict is a huge first step in
the analysis of a problem. Beyond that, prayer, sincere dialogue with the
authorities, conversations with colleagues, and discussions with consultants can provide help.

    Davida Foy Crabtree also lists several evaluative questions that may
be asked initially to encourage laity in talking about their work lives and
their faith issues.[9] In her book *The Empowering Church*, she advocates
covenant groups as a tool to support laity in their range of ministry involvements. As Christians strive to carry the presence of God into their
workplace, many will need the support of a group.

    The church should encourage its members to assess their workplace
ministries. The church should help provide the means to more closely
connect Sunday morning to Monday morning. George Peck asks a
pointed question,

    What if we worshiped and taught and enjoyed fellowship and
    prayed and managed within the life of the Christian community so

that for the majority of the week the laity could perceive themselves pursuing the mission of the gospel to the people and structures of the world around them?[10]

What if the church did that? The church and the world would be quite different. The church of Christ would be making the world a better place.

Evaluating Lay Ministry in the Church

Some have suggested that Christians currently minister too much within the walls of the church building. Many believe that Christians spend far too much time ministering to one another.

Some would call for a radical and complete surgical procedure forcing the eyes of the laity to look only to the outside of the walls of the church, rather than inside, for their ministry efforts. Such surgery, however, would devastate the church in the long run. People in church will always have needs, and the church that fails to meet those needs will quickly discover that its members lack the skills, resources, and energy needed to minister outside of the church walls. Paul told the church at Galatia, "So then, whenever we have an opportunity, let us work for the good of all, *and especially* for those of the family of faith" (Gal. 6:10, italics mine).

The Church Distinctiveness Survey, in appendix A and described in chapter 2, could give you an overall indication of the membership's perception of how well it is ministering to one another. An individual assessment of lay ministry within the church, however, might begin by again asking some evaluative questions, such as:

1. What am I specifically doing to build up the body of Christ as visibly expressed in this local congregation?
2. Do my involvements match the spiritual gifts I feel I have?
3. Do I really feel called by God to do the jobs I am doing in this church?
4. Does someone in this church have a need that no one else is addressing?
5. Could it be possible that I might be able to meet that need?

6. Did I adequately understand my task when I was asked to help?
    If not, how should I alter the job description for this responsibil-
    ity so that the next individual may be better informed?

Questions such as these and others can help an individual begin to reflect
upon her ministry within the church.

Christians should get involved only in ministries for which they
have either great interest or great skill. Too often, people are asked to
perform certain tasks or ministries with little thought to matching needs
with skills. In our church we annually distribute a list of the ministries
and open board and officer positions for the coming year and ask people
to check off those areas for which they have interest or skills. The evaluation process should start by evaluating whether or not you should ever
get involved in a ministry, not after you have already said yes.

Evaluating Lay Ministry in the Community

Ministry among church members is important, but it should never be the
primary focus for congregations. "When a church's energies are focused
on its own internal affairs and its survival, observers see these energies
withdrawn from the church's primary concern."[11] Church members need
to keep one eye toward their community as they consider ministry tasks.

Many community leaders are clamoring for churches to get more
involved in meeting the needs of their neighborhoods. I once had the
opportunity to hear Andrew Young, then mayor of Atlanta, address a
group of clergy about community ministry. He listed several ways that
the government had spent one million dollars; he continued, "If the government gave Habitat for Humanity one million dollars, they could
change the life of a community forever." Habitat for Humanity is just
one example of how a church can get involved in meeting community
needs. There are many others.

I recently asked a local community judge, Barbara Harcourt, to
name the greatest thing churches could do for our community. She responded, "Provide volunteers for Big Brothers and Big Sisters." She
went on to explain that prevention is the most cost-efficient form of stop-
ping crime. In the past some church leaders may have perceived resis-
tance from community leaders not interested in working with church

volunteers or groups, but that does not appear to be the current trend. I personally am serving on a community foundation board that is finding creative ways to encourage people to give permanently to the needs of our community. Something exciting is happening among churches and communities. They are beginning to work together to meet the needs of their people.

Just as with ministry in the workplace and ministry inside the faith community, individuals can also ask evaluative questions to assess their community ministry involvement. To evaluate a church's entire community ministry program, consult the evaluation tools described in chapter 4. The following questions are designed to help people begin to evaluate their personal community ministry involvement.

One set of evaluative questions might relate to barriers that would potentially prohibit one's maximum involvement in community ministry: What biases do I have regarding working with people, groups, government agencies, other churches, and officials in this community? How can I begin to overcome these biases? How can I listen more closely to the needs of others in this community? How can I overcome the risks associated with getting involved?

Another set of questions might assess one's experience with a community ministry: What did I learn from working with other people? Who was most helpful? Why? How can I be more helpful next time? What new skills did I learn? Were there tasks for which I had interest but didn't volunteer? What? What held me back?

A third set of questions addresses ways of telling the story to others: How can I share the meaningful moments I have had with this ministry to others? Are there opportunities in my church to tell this story? What about service clubs? What types of people would be most likely to respond to this story?

Maintaining a Balance?

Yes, a Christian may have a ministry within the workplace, the church, or the community. How does one know where to start and where to end? The answer to this question is quite different for a church than for an individual.

For an entire church, balance, in terms of ministry involvement, is the key. A church must maintain a ministry presence in its community, provide for the needs of its members, and support the ministry efforts of its members in the workplace.

But for an individual, interest and use of gifts is the key. Not every individual should try to maintain a balance among ministry in the church, the workplace, and the community. While none of these three areas should be neglected, Christians should choose to place the majority of their ministry efforts where they feel they are called and can make the greatest impact.

This chapter has dealt primarily with tools for evaluating ministry already being performed by the laity. To evaluate what ministries to get involved in, I suggest taking an individual survey-analysis of your personal spiritual gifts. The most comprehensive resource I have seen for surveying one's spiritual gifts is written by Charles Bryant, titled *Rediscovering Our Spiritual Gifts.*[12] Thomas Hawkins has also written an excellent resource specifically for the individual layperson wishing to discover personal gifts: *Claiming God's Promises, A Guide to Discovering Your Spiritual Gifts.*[13]

Epilogue

"Dad?"

"Yes."

"You know when they had everybody stand today who is a minister?"

"Yes."

"Am I a minister?"

"Yes."

"How?"

"Well. You help Zach get around at school since he can't see very well, don't you?"

"Yaa."

"Well, anytime you help someone else, you are being a minister. We were trying to show that everybody in church is the same. Even though I am the pastor, everyone in church is called to minister."

"Oh." Extended pause. "You mean like last year when they told us all of our T-Ball games were a tie, and we knew they really weren't?"

It will be difficult to convince Christians that they are all equal in

God's eyes, especially in relation to being ministers. Difficult, but necessary.

CHAPTER 7

Evaluation and Pastoral Ministry

All pastors are capable of improving their ministry competencies. Most pastors say that they desire regular improvement. Secretly tucked away in the concept of improvement, however, is the C word. That's right—CHANGE! And that's the problem!

Traditions, routines, doing the things the same old way—these can be addictive. C. S. Lewis once said that humans possess a love for the familiar. Loving the familiar way of doing things is understandable. Expecting different results from the same old way of doing things is untenable. The Alcoholics Anonymous' definition of insanity is "expecting different or better results from the same behavior."

To improve one's results, one must change. Do not be misled by false claims. Good evaluation procedures lead to suggested means for improvement, and improvement involves change. Whether the improvement involves changing behaviors, attitudes, norms, standards, or procedures, no change is implemented without some degree of difficulty. Bettering one's ministries is an arduous task. It is, however, a rewarding task.

Ninety Percent Formative and Ten Percent Summative

In chapter 4 we discussed summative program evaluation, which asks, "Is this program advancing the overall mission of this congregation?" Similarly, summative pastoral evaluation asks, "How well is this pastor or staff person advancing the overall mission of this congregation?" That's the primary question raised in the context of pastoral or staff evaluation. In chapter 4, however, we also introduced a second type of evaluation—formative. Formative pastoral evaluation asks, "What changes and enhancements can be made to aid the pastor or staff person in advancing the overall mission of this congregation?" See the difference? Summative evaluation involves discovering how well someone is doing, while formative evaluation tries to help the person improve.

A group conducting pastoral evaluation should spend 90 percent of its effort on formative evaluation. The ultimate goal of evaluation is to improve the situation for all involved. A pastor who is constantly worrying about how the results of an evaluation process will be used will find it impossible to focus creatively on possible ways of improving ministry. Jill Hudson writes, "We must consider . . . the importance of evaluation as a tool for Christian growth rather than a weapon against a perceived enemy."[1] Evaluation is not a tool for firing the pastor. Evaluation is a tool for helping the entire local congregation better accomplish the mission of God.

One way to ensure that the major focus is placed on formative rather than summative evaluation is to conduct lay evaluation simultaneously with clergy evaluation. Throughout her book *Evaluating Ministry*, Hudson advocates that "Evaluation and review are most effective when congregation and pastor are engaged in a mutual process."[2]

Another way to promote formative pastoral evaluation is to conduct evaluations at the beginning rather than at the end of the year. Dialogue about hopes and dreams for the coming year stimulates formative and limits summative evaluation.

A dialogue approach to evaluation also enhances formative evaluation. Pastoral evaluation is not something to be done to the pastor; it is something to be done with the pastor. The person being evaluated should have input at every juncture: forming the evaluation group, designing the procedure, deciding on the people to give input, analyzing the results, and mapping out a plan for improvement.

As the reader can see, there are a variety of ways to ensure that an evaluation procedure remains primarily formative rather than summative. Once accomplished, a good formative evaluation process will lead to concrete suggestions for improvement.

Improvements often can be achieved from a variety of sources. Some pastors learn new skills by attending continuing education events. Others attend a continuing education event hoping to gain a fresh insight or viewpoint into a particular need or ministry. Still others may enrich their energy from the fresh appeal of the Holy Spirit encountered at a collegial or solitary retreat.

Improvement requires change. It does not, however, require operational change. Some people improve their specific ministries by focusing more on activities deemed most important by the parishioners. Redirecting one's priorities can lead to vast improvements in one's ministry. Improvement does not always imply doing something differently. Sometimes improvement may come from seeing things differently.

Generic Pastoral Evaluation

Evaluating pastoral ministry need not be complicated. Evaluation can be conducted through the mutual analysis of several areas of ministry by a pastor or staff person and a personnel committee.

Choosing the Categories

What areas? Consider the following list:

Communication	Conflict management
Interpersonal skills	Stewardship
Pastoral care	Training volunteers
Administration	Program development
Counseling	Social ministry involvement
Spiritual development	Community involvement
Celebration and worship	Ecumenical involvement
Promotion of unity	Denominational involvement

Your group may think of other areas of ministry to include in your evaluation process. The one being evaluated should have input as categories are chosen. The specific mission of your local congregation should also play a role in choosing the categories. There may not be time to focus on every area of possible evaluation every year. Choose areas to evaluate that are most pertinent to your church and your leadership in the near future.

Gathering and Analyzing Feedback

Once certain areas from the above list have been mutually agreed upon by the pastor or staff and committee, the entire group should agree upon a period of time for the pastor or staff person to list his or her perceived strengths and weaknesses in each category. Simultaneously, the church may want to gather additional feedback on one or more of the categories from other members of the congregation. But this step is not always necessary for significant improvements to be made.

Once feedback is gathered, the pastor should discuss both revealed and self-disclosed strengths and weaknesses with the committee, and together they should brainstorm about possible avenues of improvement.

Skeptics may question, "Will a pastor ever list personal weaknesses?" Yes.

"Don't you have to survey the congregation to uncover the weaknesses of a pastor?"

Not necessarily. When a supportive environment has been created, when the pastor feels no fear or threat of being fired, when the pastor has been assured of having some control over plans for refinement, and when the focus is truly on improvement, the pastor will usually be "harder" on himself than the group involved in the formative evaluation! It is considerably more likely that someone will highlight one's own weaknesses than it is that a group will *convince* that person of such weaknesses. A group may be able to unearth the weaknesses of a pastor or staff person, but convincing a person of those weaknesses is a whole new ball game.

The Pareto principle says that 80 percent of people will perceive themselves to be in the top 20 percent of whatever category you choose. It will be extremely difficult to convince 60 percent of the people that they are not in the top 20 percent. Yet even those who perceive themselves to be in the top 20 percent are willing to admit they can improve. Most realize that there is a huge gap between being among the best and being perfect. The majority of people perceive themselves to be among the best in their profession. Very few of those people, however, view themselves as perfect. If your pastor or staff person views herself as perfect, then you have an evaluation problem beyond the scope of this book and maybe beyond the scope of reality! The bottom line is this: The key to enhancing substantive and lasting improvement in any group of personnel is to stay away from comparisons and focus on individual potential and improvement.

Designing Your Own Plan

A slightly different way of conducting an informal formative evaluation
is to ask the pastor to list several goals for the coming year from certain
areas mutually agreed upon by a lay group and the pastor. A word of
warning, however. If there is no discussion regarding the goals, the
evaluation ceases to be formative in nature. It is the discussion and potential refinement of the goals that leads the group to think about the
means of ministry improvement. Conversing about the coming year's
goals is a tool I have used. As an example, my goals for a particular year
of ministry are listed in appendix C.

There is a danger in revealing a list of future goals with a particular
group; some will be tempted to use the goals primarily as a summative
evaluation tool at the end of the year. Analyzing previously stated goals
at the end of a year can be helpful as long as the following ground rules
are set:

1. Agree to focus on means of improvement rather than on reasons
   why something was not done. The major focus should still be on
   formative rather than summative evaluation.
2. Build the discussion on a firm knowledge and understanding of
   the unique directions of your local congregation. (If the congre
   gation does not have a clear understanding of its intended future,
   refer to chapter 2.)
3. Do not compare one staff member with another or other col
   leagues.
4. Agree not to view the goals achieved as the sum of the pastor's or
   staff's accomplishments or activities during that year. Ministry is
   the most diverse profession in America, and there is no way to
   plan for all of the activities that a pastor will be involved in during a coming year. Many accomplishments may be totally unre-
   lated to any foreseeable goals at the beginning of a year.

Refrain from Reinventing the Evaluation Wheel

Some congregations and pastors may wish to conduct a more comprehensive (and formal) evaluation procedure than the generic process described above. The resources listed below will help the reader who wishes to design a more complete pastoral evaluation procedure.

A principle of this book is that every evaluation procedure should be adapted to the particular needs of a congregation. But that does not mean that your congregation needs to start from the beginning; even for a quantitative pastoral evaluation, there is no need to reinvent the evaluation wheel. Unlike lay ministry, several good evaluation models highlighting specific areas of pastoral ministry have already been formulated. It is much easier to adapt a set of evaluation procedures than to draft your own set from nothing.

Several authors have published effective and practical tools for evaluating the work of pastoral ministers. Jill Hudson presents four separate models for evaluating the work of both clergy and congregation. The evaluation process for the McKinley Church in particular provides a lengthy survey for analyzing pastoral and lay ministry.[3] *Ministry Formation for Effective Leadership* by William R. Nelson contains outstanding questions for self-reflection and theological reflection.[4] A fifty-item survey of clergy role expectations may be found in the *Handbook for Congregational Studies*.[5] The Academy of Parish Clergy has available a *Guide for Continuing Growth* that begins with an analysis of pastoral ministry.[6] In conducting an extensive evaluation of pastoral ministry, begin by reviewing previously written pastoral evaluation surveys.

Unique Churches—Unique Pastors

Just as every church is unique, so is every pastor unique in terms of background, skills, strengths, and weaknesses. Past and present role models, a pastor's seminary environment, the home congregation of a pastor, the pastor's theology and ethics professors, the spiritual development history of the pastor, the current level of moral reasoning, the personality, and the multitude of past pastoral experiences all work to make a pastor unique. And the uniqueness of pastors contributes heavily to the uniqueness of congregations.

A congregation should never expect a pastor to excel in every area of pastoral ministry. In fact, it is unequivocally impossible (I know that is redundant, but I'm really trying to make a point here) for a pastor to excel in every area of pastoral ministry. Allow me to prove it. A pastor cannot excel in every area because the strengths and weaknesses of ministry proficiencies are often linked. One source of praise for a pastor might be the cause for complaint for someone else! For example, one parishioner might be praising the creativity shown by her pastor, while someone else in the same congregation complains over that pastor's lack of regard for "standard operating procedures." Creativity and stability are always tradeoffs for an organization, and they can be for an individual as well. A forceful preacher may lack the compassion shown by a previous pastor. A pastor who appeals to the youth may lack the administrative skills exhibited by a predecessor. Realizing this phenomenon, one might be tempted to cry out, "You can't win!" I would respond, "You're right!" There will be no way to appease every parishioner. But simply realizing this fact can provide a great deal of comfort to a pastor and a great deal of insight to the group responsible for conducting the pastoral and staff evaluations.

Similar Churches—Dissimilar Staffs

Recognizing the fact that pastors contribute to the uniqueness of congregations leads to other insights and recommendations. Over time, churches will actually begin to reflect the emphases of their leaders. The personality of the church will begin to exhibit similar traits of their pastors and staff, as a result of the staff's influence. Churches that change pastors every seven or eight years will probably reflect more of their recent pastors' personalities than will churches who alter pastoral leadership every two or three years. In either case, however, churches learn to emphasize what their pastors emphasize. A caring, compassionate pastor will begin to build a caring, compassionate congregation. A prophetic and sometimes unyielding pastor will teach the congregation to do the same. In more than one case, I have witnessed a congregation show very little tolerance toward an intolerant pastor once the pastor had made what he perceived to be a minor mistake in judgment or leadership.

The personality of a congregation begins to reflect the personality of its pastors. This phenomenon is important in evaluating current pastoral staff, recommending means for improvement, and calling new staff. If, over time, churches reflect the emphases and personality of their pastoral leadership, wouldn't it be wise for a congregation to add staff with skills that complement those of the staff and pastors already serving in that congregation? Whenever a new staff person or pastor is called, this person should possess strengths in areas where the current staff is weak. This will lead to a more comprehensive ministry. Churches reflect the personalities of their pastoral leadership, so the more diverse the leadership, the more comprehensive the church's overall ministry. Lloyd Edwards advocates for this strategy. In his book *How We Belong, Fight, and Pray,* he shows how personality type affects church life.[7]

Staff members should complement one another and be evaluated with these biases in mind. Staff members should never be evaluated against the strengths of one another. Rather, staff members should be evaluated against the weaknesses of one another! A church should celebrate the fact that each staff person does not preach in the same manner, visit with the same effectiveness, or manage with the same attention to detail. The different strengths among the staff should be carefully noted and celebrated within the overall mission of a local congregation.

Epilogue

My daughter, Kelsey, was almost out the door on the last day of kindergarten before Christmas vacation, when she voluntarily recited the instructions for the day. She had apparently filtered the instructions from her teacher through her mind and felt the need to go over them prior to leaving for school.

"Everyone is to bring a boy gift or a girl gift valued from two to five dollars," she began, "then they play music, and when the music stops, that's your gift, and we have to say thank you even though we won't like what we get."

That is not bad advice for evaluation. Accentuate the positive. Begin with the strengths and, only then, move on toward the negatives. Always keep your cool, even when you don't like what you hear. Never try to convince someone that you have already received this piece of information before. Always say thank you, even when you have no intention of using the advice delivered.

CHAPTER 8

The Experts Respond to Dilemmas

When presented on paper, evaluation can appear to be a simple task.

It is always a different story in the real world. It is never easy to turn principle into praxis, especially in the field of evaluation. On the other hand, knowledge of a particular field prior to practicing in the field has never been a detriment.

This chapter opens the door to application of some of the principles already presented in this book. I'll present four church dilemmas related to the field of evaluation. The dilemmas have no one right solution. As each scenario is unraveled, take time to ponder the situation yourself. Brainstorm about how you might approach the problem. You may find that a principle of evaluation presented earlier in this text readily comes to mind as a way of approaching the problem. (I wonder if all authors have these grandiose expectations of their writing?) You probably will approach the problem with your usual problem-solving skills but with an approach or attitude about evaluation influenced by the tone of this book. (I refuse to give up all hope that this book has made a difference.)

I have asked experts in the field of church evaluation to respond to each dilemma. And I also give some commentary on the dilemmas. Try to respond to the dilemmas yourself, prior to reading the responses from the experts.

The three experts are Roy Oswald, a full-time consultant for The Alban Institute; Jill Hudson, a Presbyterian denominational executive; and Paul Light, a denominational researcher for American Baptist Churches, USA. I am grateful to these people for supplying their insights into these problems.

Dilemma Number 1

A church that uses its own personnel to evaluate every program and ministry runs the risk of never asking the critical questions that only an outsider can ask. But a church that enlists the help of an external evaluator runs the risk of the evaluator never fully understanding the unique situation of this particular congregation. When should a congregation enlist the help of an outside evaluation consultant?

All of the experts agreed that there are times when congregations should enlist the help of an evaluation consultant. Roy Oswald contends that an outside consultant "signals to the congregation that the decision makers are taking a process seriously." Each expert suggested a somewhat different set of stimuli for bringing in an outside consultant.

Paul Light suggested two factors that require the help of a consultant. "The first factor," he asserts, "is the level of conflict or controversy about a particular program or ministry. A consultant . . . can help design the evaluation, gather the information, and interpret the results in ways that creatively deal with the conflict." I concur that many conflicts are more easily analyzed by "fresh eyes." Whether the conflict arises in a relationship, a group, or an entire congregation, myopia can set in quickly. Roy Oswald agrees that an outside consultant can help in a troubled situation and adds, "It often takes an outside facilitator to bring groups of people together to begin to talk clearly and candidly with one another."

Light suggests a second factor that should prompt outside consultation: "the amount of time, energy, and commitment that one or more persons have invested in the program or ministry. When persons feel a lot is at stake in their work, an evaluation of results runs a higher risk of becoming a personal condemnation." Light points out the dangers of performing summative evaluations and suggests that this might be an excellent time to enlist the help of a consultant, especially when extensive work has been put into the program.

Jill Hudson suggests another point where outside evaluation can be helpful—in the case of a long pastorate. "If ministers truly listen to discern God's will for their life, an outside consultant can help in gaining useful feedback which might assist the pastor in determining whether he or she has remaining work to do in this setting or whether it's time to move on. If a pastor remains, the outside evaluation should have put in proper perspective what is going well and what might need additional attention." Hudson feels a consultant can effectively help pastors sort out future directions. No matter how long a pastor's tenure, suggests Oswald, when role renegotiation is involved, an outside consultant is a good idea.

Outside consultants can help not only pastors, but also congregations, set goals for the future, contend both Hudson and Oswald.

Hudson is a big fan of periodic comprehensive review of a congregation's ministry. She suggests bringing in an outside consultant just prior to establishing a new set of long-range goals.

Oswald complements Hudson, advocating for the two-step process of an overall ministry evaluation with an outside consultant first and long-range planning second, recommending that the consultant guide the congregation through both phases of analysis and planning. Oswald explains his proposal:

> I would recommend that an in-depth process be engaged once every four or five years. A significant portion of the congregation should be engaged in this evaluation. Basically congregational members should be asked what they like about the current ministry of the congregation and what are some of their key concerns. This evaluation should then be followed by a strategic planning process. An outside facilitator can often be a catalyst in bringing the energy of the congregation to examine its life and to plan where it wants to go in the future.

Dilemma Number 2

A particular church has had a volunteer serve in the same position for thirty-five years. Many in the congregation have suggested that it's time for a change in this position. Someone recently suggested, "Why not do an evaluation of this person's particular ministry?" That suggestion led to the church contacting you for advice. What specific issues would you suggest that this church address as they approach this problem?

The three experts took different approaches to the problem. Yet all three had some similarities, suggesting that the church find a new place for the volunteer to serve and celebrate the work of the volunteer.

Light diagrammed a process for handling the problem. He first analyzed the issues as (1) honoring with integrity the work of this volunteer, (2) providing help for the volunteer to evaluate the work done, (3) providing both continuity and change in the work as an evaluation suggests, and (4) providing other avenues of service for the volunteer, if evaluation suggests a change. He then outlined a five-step process:

1. Create a team of three to four people including a pastor to meet with the volunteer to do two things: design a way for the church to honor and celebrate the work of the volunteer and to design an evaluation of the results of that work.
2. Involve the volunteer in all phases of the evaluation.
3. Emphasize to the congregation the positive aspects of the findings of the evaluation.
4. Discuss all aspects of the findings in sessions of the team with the volunteer.
5. Discuss with the volunteer any proposed changes stemming from the evaluation before they are presented to committees or the congregation.

Oswald analyzed the bigger picture behind this dilemma. He suggests a solution that gets at the root of this problem so it will not happen again. He advocates for a bylaw change to indicate that volunteers can hold a particular role for only so many years. He acknowledges, however, that this solution solves one problem and creates another, "The problem it may cause is too high a turnover of volunteers, so there is not a whole lot of in-depth work volunteers are able to do in any given position."

Oswald suggests that congregations establish a coordinator of volunteers or a task force on volunteerism. "This person or group would see to it that people are well placed in roles that give them great satisfaction. The key to effective volunteer ministries is the fact that volunteer roles are evaluated periodically."

Oswald says a policy of written job descriptions for volunteers could have prevented this problem.

When you have a written job description and the volunteer is clearly not performing up to the standards of that job, the volunteer needs to be confronted by the volunteer coordinator or committee and given an opportunity either to meet the standards or find another volunteer role.

"The way to fire a volunteer," Oswald proposes, "is to find out what else they would like to do and to move them into a volunteer role that much better suits their time and talents."

Hudson took a different approach to the problem. She offered the following commentary:

> I do not believe evaluation is the key here. It does no good to look at the current performance of a faithful servant of thirty-five years and suddenly say, "Your work isn't up to par, good-bye." Instead, I would recommend approaching this from the perspective of "Who will replace you when you're gone? We need to be training new leadership for your position and would ask you to co-serve with a person for one year in order to assist this person in accepting the new responsibility." Use the more seasoned volunteer as "coach." Do not be afraid of passing on bad habits. Generally, new volunteers are mature enough to know that when they are on their own, they can do it differently. Lean on the volunteer's understanding that others should have the opportunity to give to the church just as she has, and now it's time to prepare them for that. A big celebration of the volunteer's ministry in this area goes a long way in soothing the loss. Find another helpful job for the volunteer to do quickly so that he or she does not feel put out to pasture. This is not an area for "evaluation"; it's an area for pastoral decisions.

However one chooses to handle such a dilemma, keep in mind the principle discussed in chapter 7: It is unlikely that one person will convince another that he or she is not performing well. Evaluation, aimed at this goal, will probably fail. Any evaluation procedure that addresses a problem similar to this volunteer scenario should allow the issues to emerge from the one being evaluated; do not try to force the person to see something that others perceive to be a problem.

Dilemma Number 3

At a recent worship committee meeting, someone suggested adding a second worship service for the summer. The idea received positive feedback from everyone in attendance, although the members gave little input regarding the format of such a service. Summer is only one month away; it would be helpful for this congregation to receive some evaluative information regarding this idea. Due to time constraints, the worship committee feels compelled to choose between interviewing and surveying. Which would you suggest and why?

All three experts clearly delineated the differing results obtained from quantitative versus qualitative evaluation. Each expert agreed that a combination of the two is best if time allows. Several quantitative and qualitative evaluation procedures were discussed in chapter 3. Additional ideas were conveyed by our experts.

Light clarified the different outcomes that can be obtained from the two types of evaluation in this way, "A good survey will produce a breadth of information (quantitative) while a good interview process will produce a depth of information (qualitative)." The decision regarding which method to choose rests, in Light's mind, on whether depth or breadth is preferred. "Would it be more helpful for us to know the depth of feelings about the issues held by a small number of the congregation, or the general range of responses of the whole congregation?"

Acknowledging that a committee might not know the answer to this question, Light gave a little more insight:

> If the committee feels that they need help in designing the second service and/or they need commitments from others to participate in leading or promoting the service, the interview process would be preferred. If the second service will be much like the first service, however, and the time that the service is held is the only major difference, a survey can tell the committee how many in the congregation would prefer optional times for a second service.

Hudson suggested a way that both qualitative and quantitative information could be obtained within a limited time frame:

> I would recommend that five to six standard interviewing questions

be developed and that telephone interviews of no more than twenty minutes be held with a list of "key" leaders in the congregation. Additionally, an open forum could be held that would have a survey instrument distributed and completed in the same setting. Survey forms could be available in the church office for those who request them and are unable to attend. I'd put a two-week time table on the data gathering and go with what you get. The people who are most interested are likely the people you'll be serving so I wouldn't worry about those who do not respond.

Oswald suggested a nontraditional format for gathering information called "open space technology":

> In this particular process you call a congregational meeting and try to have as many of your members come out as possible. You then begin to have them walk to different parts of the room based upon questions that you ask. For example, those who would favor contemporary music in the second service should walk to one side of the room. Those who would favor traditional music walk to another side of the room, etc. In a two-hour period, you can ask a whole series of questions and have people continue to walk to different parts of the room based upon how they respond. This approach gets people involved in the data as it is emerging.

Dilemma Number 4

A pastor of a congregation would like to form a group constructively to evaluate her preaching ministry. She enjoys preaching and personally believes that this is one of her stronger attributes. She also believes that even the strongest gift can be improved. What suggestions would you offer in conducting this evaluation?

Several similarities emerged from the experts' suggestions about sermon evaluations, including the involvement of a "team," the development of a checklist for what to look for while evaluating, contracting for a specified period of time, and eventually including diverse respondents.

The suggested lengths of time for the evaluations differed among the experts. Hudson recommended twelve weeks. Oswald recommended two times for each homogeneous group, using diverse groups over time.

Each expert added a unique flavor to his or her proposed method of evaluating sermons. Hudson advocated for a "mystery person" to be added to the evaluation team.

> I would suggest an evaluation team of two people chosen by the pastor, two people chosen by the governing board and one "mystery" listener each week. The mystery listener would be recruited by one of the team members to listen for *that* Sunday only. A listening guide could be developed (example: use of contemporary illustrations, eye contact, animated delivery, etc.) which would be used by all. The group would listen each week and evaluate that Sunday's sermon. The last Sunday of each month they would meet with the pastor and give feedback from their notes on each of the areas being evaluated. Goals for growth would be established at each meeting and progress would be evaluated at the next. At the end of the agreed upon time, the group could assist the pastor in any decisions regarding education opportunities in the area of preaching.

Oswald's approach centered around developing homogeneous teams that would meet with the pastor once prior to the sermon and once following the sermon. Prior to the sermon, the group discusses what it views as the issues of the text and what questions it wants answered. Immediately following the sermon, the same group meets to talk about its evaluation. The goal in Oswald's scenario differed somewhat from the other two experts. The goal for Oswald's process appeared to be to allow the preacher to discern the various needs that she should attend to during a sermon.

Groups might first be formed around various age groups. The pastor might begin by meeting with a group of young people, then middle-aged people, and so on, until the pastor understands the needs of various groups within her congregation.

Another way to organize the groups, Oswald suggested, might be around personality temperaments.[1] This would involve meeting, over time, with a group from each of the four Myers-Briggs temperaments of sensing/judging, intuitive/feeling, sensing/perceiving, and intuitive/thinking. "It is indeed challenging to try to preach to all four temperaments," Oswald says, "but I believe this would significantly improve the preaching of the pastor."

The better understanding a pastor has of parishioners, the better that person will be able to preach among those parishioners. See the November-December 1993 issue of *Congregations* for two short surveys to help pastors discern the needs of congregants to better preach to their needs.[2]

Light offered several practical suggestions for the evaluation team: clarifying who will lead the discussion and what the pastor's role in the discussion will be; explaining the methodology before the group meets; talking about how to receive the information with a spirit of acceptance and gratitude; and making it clear the preaching is not being "graded" by the team.

Epilogue

For Christmas one year, my son received a calculator that doubled as a game. If you pushed the addition button first, the calculator would flash two numbers for the user to add. My son was showing the gift to a friend visiting our house. My daughter also had a friend visiting, and she and her friend began playing with the calculator when the boys finished. The younger girls performed well for the first couple of problems. Then the calculator asked them to add five plus nine, much larger numbers than they had previously added.

"I know," said Kelsey. "You put up nine fingers. I'll put up five and count with my other hand." They proceeded to team together to get the answer, the entire calculation being performed while they rocked side by side in Kelsey's favorite chair.

Evaluation dilemmas are similar in effect. Sometimes old ways just don't work anymore. Sometimes even new ways won't work without the help of a friend.

CHAPTER 9

Who are we when we are not doing anything?

Church evaluation involves finding out how a local church can better accomplish the mission that God has presented to that specific congregation. In previous chapters, I have presented ways to analyze the work of the laity, the pastoral staff, renewal efforts, and programs. There is one more arena to cover. The congregation can also evaluate the influence it is having when the church is not gathered together in any official capacity.

Understanding the Issue

Every church should occasionally ask, "Who are we when we are not doing anything?" In other words, "Who are we when we are not officially deciding, programming, playing together, singing, worshipping, evangelizing, or working on anything?"

A Classic Illustration

An illustration by Herbert Simon helps to pose this intriguing question.[1] Hora and Tempus were watchmakers. The watches made by each man contained one thousand parts. Their work was occasionally interrupted by people telephoning them to place orders. If the phone rang while Tempus was constructing a watch, he had to lay down the watch causing it to fall apart; after the phone call he had to start assembling all over again, from the beginning. Hora, on the other hand, designed his construction so that he could put watches together in subassemblies of ten parts each. Ten of the subassemblies could be assembled into a larger subassembly and the ten larger subassemblies could be assembled into a complete watch. Phone ringing did not occur that frequently. There was only a one-in-one-hundred chance that either would be interrupted while adding a piece; even so, because of Tempus' lack of subassemblies, it took him four thousand times as long as Hora to construct a watch.

Tempus was concerned only about the completed product. Many churches are the same way. Some committees live from committee meeting to committee meeting, seemingly oblivious to what else has happened in the church during that period. Some churches carry on traditions such as Friend Days or hanging of the greens with little or no thought to what has happened since the last time the tradition was celebrated. They are concerned only with the completed product, not with the components—happenings that might play a huge part in this year's celebration.

But productive Hora was concerned about the different components that made up the watch. A parish parallel? An organization needs to pay attention to what is happening in between its official gatherings. A great deal can take place in a church between worship services, between committee and board meetings, between Easters, Christmases, Friend Days, and sabbaticals.

When Are the "Down Times"?

What happens to your church when everybody goes home after Saturday evening or Sunday morning worship? What happens to your church when the pastor takes a three-week vacation? What happens when all of the church staff members attend a national convention or conference? What happens to your church during the summer when key people vacation for extended periods? What happens to your church when people leave for the South during the winter or North during the summer? Is anything happening in between the times of worship? How long does it take your church to "jump start" again after a new pastor or staff person has been called?

Interaction Is the Key

What allowed Hora to construct so many more watches than Tempus was a tighter interaction of parts at the lower end of the assembly process. Most organizations, including churches, have a tight interaction among the people at the top of the organization. While staff meetings are common, only rarely do all of the people in the organization interact in a significant manner in various subgroups. What is happening to the church in between the larger gatherings of interactions among the members? Who is the church when the church is not doing anything as an entire complete unit?

There may be vast activity in the subsystems of churches, but the activity may not be advancing the intended mission of that local congregation. The social grapevine, or communication network, may or may not be working toward the same ends as the church's "official units." Many programs are sabotaged by one person or a few people who are hard at work even when the rest of the church does not appear to be doing anything. Often a church pays little attention to its informal networks because it assumes not much is happening in these networks.

The Continuous Cycle of Information

But a great deal can be happening. Weick's concept of "causal loops" reveals much can take place in the social communication network of a church.[2] Here's an example of how causal loops work. If you have ever sat in a meeting and experienced boredom, you have probably experienced a causal loop. As your level of boredom went up, the number of ideas you thought of decreased. As the number of ideas you thought of decreased, your willingness to make a comment decreased. As your willingness to make a comment decreased, your self-consciousness decreased. As your self-consciousness decreased, your understanding of the discussion decreased. As your understanding of the discussion decreased, your level of boredom increased—completing the first lap of a continuing loop. If the above loop is left alone, the person eventually falls out of his chair or is shunned or condemned or mocked by peers for snoring.

This causal loop illustration involved an individual. You can probably quickly identify a causal loop that applies to the informal communication

network in your church. Left alone, without the attention of anyone outside the loop, a loop can escalate and cause much damage very quickly;
activity in the "silent loops" of a church often advance without the attention of others. Somervill declares, "Churches often get into more
trouble than corporations by assuming that time will heal all wounds."[3]

Gathering Data to Improve the Situation

There is no *easy* way to analyze this type of informal church activity, but
it can be done. One way is to "hang out" where the locals hang out and
keep an ear to the conversations in the room. Bring up a particular ministry in your church and see if anyone knows about it. You will probably
receive additional information about your church as well. Information
regarding how your church is perceived by people who live in the neighborhood and community can be very helpful.

There is also a way to analyze the communication patterns of your
congregation. For a specified period of time, such as two weeks, ask a
certain group of church leaders or staff members to keep track of whom
they converse with. If people are willing to reveal the broad nature of
the conversations, you will be able to track even the flow of ideas within
your congregation.

You can also conduct a power analysis to evaluate the invisible influence that some congregants knowingly or unknowingly have over
others. Roy Oswald has authored a resource to analyze both your personal level of power and the corporate power within your congregation.
The book also encourages readers to come to grips with a personal theology of power.[4]

People are not the only source of activity between a congregation's
official gatherings. Conduct an analysis of your church's visual material. What messages are sent by your church's printed matter? What is
on your bulletin boards? What do your banners convey? Are there
posters up? Where? What do they say? Are the pictures inclusive?
Inclusive in what respects? Are the messages conveyed consistent with
the image you would like to present?

It is helpful for a church to ask, "Who are we when we are not formally doing anything?" Between official gatherings, what is taking
place to advance your congregation's proposed mission? What is taking
place to inhibit your proposed mission?

Evaluate your current situation—this very week. Have you given your members any material to read or reflect or focus on before you gather again in an official way? Were your members invited to do something as a result of your last worship service? Will there be any accountability for their actions?

Take one week and pay attention to every single thing that happens in your congregation's life. Allow your senses to be inundated with the signs, symbols, and signals of your church both in and out of activity. The church should take a look at itself in times of worship, gatherings of business meetings, Bible study discussions, and times of crisis. The church also should take a look at itself during times of no formal activity.

Accomplishing the ministry that God has given to a local congregation is a difficult task. It will not be done without evaluating every aspect of church life to identify new and better ways to contribute to God's mission. Develop an "evaluator's eye" toward your congregation. Be a person who consistently helps your church live out its specific role in the kingdom of God.

Epilogue

I will always remember Brandon's first difficult spelling test. He had done well on the few tests he'd previously taken. Then he brought home a list that breathed fear into his eyes. Two of the words, *children* and *teacher,* were extremely long. "Twice as long as any other words I've ever had!" he exclaimed. It was the sheer magnitude of the words that intimidated him. We practiced. He wrote the words. He spelled them aloud. He dreamed about them.

Friday came. Test day. After school he walked proudly through the door displaying yet another "A+." Then I glanced at the top of his paper. He had spelled every word right on his list, but had misspelled his name. It was not marked. Maybe Mrs. Pitts had missed it. Or, maybe, she had been generous to my son.

I encourage you: As you begin to evaluate your congregational life, apply many of the theories and insights contained in this book. But never neglect the little things that will continue to spell out who you are as a congregation.

Church Distinctiveness Survey

A means for constructing a profile of the qualitative distinctiveness of your church

Please rate the following nine dimensions of church distinctiveness according to the importance you believe is currently placed upon each dimension in your church. Each dimension probably exists to some degree within the life of your congregation. However, you are to rate each dimension in terms of its relative importance to the other dimensions.

Please read all nine descriptions first. Then return and rate each description by drawing on your perceptions, experiences, and observations. Rate each dimension according to the following scale:

1——————————————————————————————10

Of least importance   Of greatest importance

ADORATION   scale value _____

Praising God for all of God's love, power, care, and presence displayed in the world is a special emphasis in the church. The adoration of God for who God is, for what God has done, and for what God promises to do in the future is talked about and celebrated in both corporate worship and individual lives. Glorifying God extends beyond the sanctuary to the classrooms, the committee meetings, and every aspect of programming.

BENEVOLENT   scale value _____

The church has a special commitment to foster a humane environment.
It continually strives to create a capacity for caring, compassion, and
empathy to all people, especially those outside the church membership.
The church readily responds both emotionally and financially to the
needs of others, whether they arise in the community or across the world.

COGNITIVE   scale value _____

The church has a strong commitment to increase the knowledge and
understanding of God. Developing a theology, recognizing the continuing revelation of God, comprehending scripture, and becoming familiar
with doctrine, are all emphasized in the church.

CONSECRATION   scale value _____

The church has a special commitment to personal involvement with God.
It stresses the need for a relationship with God and makes available opportunities for each person to expand a personal relationship with God in
a variety of ways. The work of the Holy Spirit, prayer groups, and the
need to live without sin in our everyday lives—these are all central to the
life of the church.

ECUMENICAL   scale value _____

The church displays a major commitment to working with churches of
other backgrounds, denominations, and faiths. This commitment is evi-
denced through work projects, personal contacts, respect of differences,
and desires to expand involvement and understanding of other churches.
The church sets an example of Christian unity.

EVANGELISTIC   scale value _____

Every member of the congregation is committed to reaching the unchurched. The need for sharing the gospel is emphasized in all phases of
programming. The members of the church are eager to share the gospel
with strangers and friends and to send resources to witness to peoples in
all parts of the world.

MINISTRY TO MEMBERS   scale value _____

The church has a major commitment to ministering to the members of
the congregation. Whether members are in need of counseling, financial
help, friendship, visitation in the home or hospital, the need rarely goes
unmet. Members emphasize becoming well-acquainted; this allows new
needs to be readily recognized.

STEWARDSHIP   scale value _____

The church displays a sincere commitment to gather and use resources
in an efficient and effective manner. Members are actively involved in
committing their finances, spiritual gifts, natural abilities, and time
toward the direction of God's leading. The church is also a competent
trustee of its building and property.

TRADITION   scale value _____

The church has a special commitment to the importance of its heritage in
interpreting the issues that arise within the church and society. The
church is committed to an understanding of its religious, biblical, denominational, and community roots and to preserving and transmitting
this heritage. The church is also committed toward understanding today's issues that will become tomorrow's heritage. To do this it remains
informed of current denominational, community, world, and religious
issues.

This survey first appeared in Christian Ministry, January-February 1991. It was written by Dr. C. Jeff Woods (431 W US 52, Rushville, IN 46173) and reproduced with permission from The Alban Institute, Inc. (Suite 433 North, 4550 Montgomery Avenue, Bethesda, MD 20814.) Copyright 1995. All rights reserved, however, readers are granted permission to copy it for use in their churches.

Church Renewal Diagnosis Instrument

A means for constructing a church renewal strategy for your congregation through the avenues of awakening, reformation, and mission

Every church could benefit from emphasizing renewal. This survey is designed to help your church match a renewal strategy to the specific character of your church. Below are statements related to the way a church operates, worships, makes decisions, carries out its programs, and so forth. Give your view of how things are in your church right now. For some of the items you may feel that your impression is not well informed. Answer anyway. Your individual viewpoint is very important. In the blank beside each item, write the number that best represents your opinion from the following scale:

0	1	2	3	4	5	6
Don't Know	Strongly Disagree	Disagree	Sort of Disagree	Sort of Agree	Agree	Strongly Agree

_____ 1. Our church is a vibrant place.

_____ 2. Our church has an up-to-date constitution.

_____ 3. Our church is involved in many ministries.

_____   4. Our church could use a good revival.

_____   5. It takes a long time for a ministry to get underway in our church.

_____   6. Our church is not very involved in the community.

_____   7. Our pastor often stresses renewal.

_____   8. I seldom get bored at a church business meeting.

_____   9. Our church is well-known for meeting needs in this community.

_____   10. Our church leadership should be more in tune with God.

_____   11. Our church has resisted changing for years.

_____   12. Our church needs to reach out more to people in our neighborhood.

_____   13. God is surely leading our church.

_____   14. Our church is very open to change.

_____   15. I could easily explain our church's role in our community.

_____   16. Very little emphasis is placed upon the Spirit of God in our church.

_____   17. Our church approaches issues the same way it did thirty years ago.

_____   18. Our church is not meeting the needs of some in our church family.

_____   19. People in our church talk regularly about what God is doing in their lives.

_____ 20. Our church has kept up with the times.

_____ 21. People in the community know what ministries our church offers.

_____ 22. Our church desperately needs to be renewed.

_____ 23. Our church members often say, "We've never done it like that before," to stifle a new idea.

_____ 24. There are very few opportunities to minister to others at my workplace.

_____ 25. Most of our church members practice a daily devotional time with God.

_____ 26. There are very few barriers in our church for people who are different from us.

_____ 27. Our pastor regularly talks about mission.

_____ 28. God needs to send our church a wake-up call.

_____ 29. Many things need updating in our congregation.

_____ 30. Our church may give to mission, but we don't do mission very well.

_____ 31. God is very visible in our church.

_____ 32. I like the way our church gets things done.

_____ 33. The community knows that our church cares for them.

_____ 34. I'm not sure I know what church renewal is.

_____ 35. Our church has too many committees that do very little.

_____ 36. Mission should be more of a priority in our church.

_____ 37. Our church is on the right track with God.

_____ 38. There is not much wrong with our church procedures.

_____ 39. Mission is what really binds our church together.

_____ 40. People in this church are starving for God.

_____ 41. Our church could learn a lot from a management consultant.

_____ 42. We do a lot more socializing than we do ministering.

_____ 43. I get closer to God every time I come to church.

_____ 44. Our church appeals very much to today's people.

_____ 45. Our church does a good job of ministering to each other.

_____ 46. Our church should do a better job of helping people discover God.

_____ 47. Our church pretty much does things the way they have always been done.

_____ 48. We need to do more ministry ourselves, rather than leaving it all up to the pastoral staff.

_____ 49. Our church offers many opportunities for people to deepen their spirituality.

_____ 50. Overall, our church is ready for the next century.

_____ 51. If someone in our church has a need, we readily respond.

_____ 52. Our church members need to get closer to God.

_____ 53. Our church structure often gets in the way of what we should be doing as a church.

_____ 54. Very few of our church members consider themselves to be ministers.

Directions for Scoring

Scoring Key

1._____	4._____	2._____	5._____	3._____	6._____
7._____	10._____	8._____	11._____	9._____	12._____
13._____	16._____	14._____	17._____	15._____	18._____
19._____	22._____	20._____	23._____	21._____	24._____
25._____	28._____	26._____	29._____	27._____	30._____
31._____	34._____	32._____	35._____	33._____	36._____
37._____	40._____	38._____	41._____	39._____	42._____
43._____	46._____	44._____	47._____	45._____	48._____
49._____	52._____	50._____	53._____	51._____	54._____

Total: _____	_____	_____	_____	_____	_____
(A1)	(A2)	(R1)	(R2)	(M1)	(M2)

Transfer your answers to the questions in the blanks above. Add up the numbers for each column and write down the total for each column.

To calculate your awakening indicator, subtract the total for column 2 (A2) from the total for column 1 (A1).

To calculate your reformation indicator, subtract the total for column 4 (R2) from the total for column 3 (R1).

To calculate your mission indicator, subtract the total for column 6 (M2) from the total for column 5 (M1).

(A1) – (A2)   =_____Awakening Indicator
(R1) – (R2)   =_____Reformation Indicator
(M1) – (M2)   =_____Mission Indicator

Your three indicators reveal the relative strengths of these three paths to renewal that exist in every congregation. Each indicator may be a positive or negative number. The highest number represents what you perceive to be the strongest path to renewal in your church. The lowest number represents what you perceive to be the weakest path to renewal in your church.

(Reproduced with permission from The Alban Institute, Inc., Suite 433 North, 4550 Montgomery Avenue, Bethesda, MD 20814. Copyright 1995. All rights reserved.)

Directions for Groups or Leaders

You may want to average the responses from several members to obtain a composite view of the three indicators. You may want to compare perceptions of the three indicators among various groups in your church. Some congregations may wish to devise a renewal strategy that focuses on their weakest path to renewal. Other congregations may wish to begin by building on their strengths.

This instrument is only one measurement of these three paths to renewal. The information revealed to you through this instrument should be integrated with other information about your church.

(Survey written by Dr. C. Jeff Woods, 1431 W. US 52, Rushville, IN 46173)

Annual Ministry Goals for Rev. C. Jeff Woods

Administration

1. Hold a planning meeting involving people from all the church boards.

2. Train four laypeople to preach a sermon during the month of October.

3. Work with groups to plan at least two retreats.

4. Seek out continuing education opportunities for laity.

5. Give input to the church boards.

6. Promote resources for laity. Look for opportunities for laity to use their skills in our church, other churches, the denomination, and the community.

7. Work with a group to plan the Friendship Hall dedication.

8. Encourage members to reach out to minorities in our community, possibly involving a Sunday school class in an exchange with another congregation.

9. Oversee the implementation of Friend Day.

10. Oversee the tithing emphasis task force.

Leadership in Ministry

1. Lead a weekly afternoon and evening Bible study.

2. Counsel members and nonmembers who request counseling including premarital couples; make referrals as necessary.

3. Be available to substitute teach for Sunday school teachers.

Worship Leading

1. Plan sermon titles and topics three months in advance to aid the choir director and strive for a balance of issues.

2. Emphasize variety in the evening worship services—experiential worship, sermons, concerts, video, and guest speakers.

3. With the approval of the deacons, schedule guest speakers when away from the pulpit.

4. Emphasize lay ministry "eight to five," including a sermon series on lay ministry.

5. Enhance the church procedures for baptism and baby dedication.

Visitation

1. Visit people in their home a day or two before any scheduled surgery.

2. Visit people whenever they are in the hospital for an extended stay or in their home following a hospital stay.

3. Visit members in their homes in the priority of: (1) crisis, (2) church business, (3) homebound, (4) elderly, (5) fellowship.

Representation

1. Represent the church in the local Rush County Ministerial Association and serve in rotation with the other ministers in meeting the needs for radio devotions, nursing home worship services (Wednesdays in December), and hospital chaplaincy.

2. Represent our church and others on the general board of American Baptist Churches and report back to our church and other churches in the district. Serve on the executive committee of the general board and chair the "policy statements and resolutions committee" of the general board.

3. Represent the church in dealings with the American Baptist Churches of Indiana and report informational items back to appropriate bodies.

Service

1. Serve as a mentor for two members in the Certified Lay Ministry Program.

2. Serve as a consultant to the president of Habitat for Humanity in Rush County (a member of the congregation).

3. Conduct an evaluation of the annual meeting of the American Baptist Churches of Indiana.

4. Be available as a member of the commission for review of ministerial standing.

5. Serve on the "Renewed for Mission" task force for American Baptist Churches of Indiana.

Personal

1. Seek daily renewal by maintaining a spiritual discipline.

2. Maintain contact with ministerial support groups including the Indiana American Baptist pastors, Rush County Ministerial Association, and Academy of Parish Clergy.

3. Read at least twelve books from a variety of fields that will benefit my total ministry.

4. Take the allotted vacation time during the coming year and use the time to build relationships within my immediate family.

5. Participate in two continuing education events that benefit some aspect of my ministry.

6. Continue to write for publication.

NOTES

Chapter 1

1. Egon G. Guba and Yvonna S. Lincoln, *Effective Evaluation* (San Francisco: Jossey-Bass, 1983), 1.
2. Ralph Tyler, *Basic Principles of Curriculum and Instruction* (Chicago: University of Chicago Press, 1950).
3. D. L. Stufflebeam, et al., *Educational Evaluation and Decision-Making* (Itasca, Ill.: Peacock, 1971).
4. Michael Scriven, "Pros and Cons about Goal-Free Evaluation," *Evaluation Comment* 3 (1974): 1-4.
5. R. E. Stake, *Evaluating the Arts in Education: A Responsive Approach* (Columbus, Ohio: Merrill, 1975).

Chapter 2

1. Loren Mead, *The Once and Future Church* (Bethesda, Md.: The Alban Institute, 1991), 24-27.
2. Loren Mead, *More Than Numbers: The Ways Churches Grow* (Bethesda, Md.: The Alban Institute, 1993), 13.
3. Ibid., 1.
4. Carl S. Dudley and Sally A. Johnson, *Energizing the Congregation: Images That Shape Your Church's Ministry* (Louisville: Westminster/John Knox Press, 1993), 110-111.
5. C. Jeff Woods, "Surveying to Find a Church's Distinctiveness," *Christian Ministry* 22, no. 1 (January-February 1991): 11-14.

Chapter 3

1. Richard A. Berk and Peter H. Rossi, *Thinking about Program Evaluation* (Newbury Park, Calif.: Sage, 1990), 35.
2. Egon G. Guba and Yvonna S. Lincoln, *Effective Evaluation* (San Francisco: Jossey-Bass, 1983), 227.
3. Ibid., 231.
4. Jackson Carroll, Carl Dudley, and William McKinney, eds., *Handbook for Congregational Studies* (Nashville: Abingdon Press, 1986).
5. Jill Hudson, *Evaluating Ministry* (Bethesda, Md.: The Alban Institute, 1992), 19-21.
6. Roy Oswald and Speed Leas, *The Inviting Church* (Bethesda, Md.: The Alban Institute, 1987).
7. Duncan McIntosh and Richard Rusbuldt, *Planning Growth in Your Church* (Valley Forge, Pa.: Judson Press, 1983), 177-180.

Chapter 4

1. David C. Laubach, "Invite-a-Friend Sunday," *The Good News Link* 13 (1990): 1. (This is a newsletter of Board of National Ministries, American Baptist Churches, USA).
2. Richard A. Berk and Peter H. Rossi, *Thinking about Program Evaluation* (Newbury Park, Calif.: Sage, 1990), 14.
3. Ibid.
4. Egon G. Guba and Yvonna S. Lincoln, *Effective Evaluation* (San Francisco: Jossey-Bass, 1983), 40.
5. C. Peter Wagner, *Leading Your Church to Growth* (Ventura, Calif.: Regal Books, 1984), 46-62.
6. Ibid., 63-70.

Chapter 5

1. Duncan McIntosh and Richard Rusbuldt, *Planning Growth in Your Church* (Valley Forge, Pa.: Judson Press, 1983).
2. Donald Fothergill, "A Leader's Manual for Renewing Mainline Churches" (D.Min. project, Fuller Theological Seminary, 1982).

3. Howard Snyder, *Signs of the Spirit: How God Reshapes the Church* (Grand Rapids: Zondervan, 1989).

4. Lyle Schaller, *The Local Church Looks to the Future* (Nashville: Abingdon Press, 1968).

5. Daniel Buttry, *Bringing Your Church Back to Life* (Valley Forge, Pa.: Judson Press, 1988).

6. Donald Maxam, "The Church Renewal Movement in Sociological Perspective," *Review of Religious Research* 23, no. 2 (1981): 196.

7. James I. Packer, "Steps to the Renewal of the Christian People," in *Summons to Faith and Renewal*, ed. Peter S. Williamson and Kevin Perrotta (Ann Arbor: Servant, 1983), 108.

8. See Owen D. Owens, *Covenant Prayer Group Manual* (Valley Forge, Pa.: Church and Community Development, American Baptist Churches, USA, 1988).

9. See James Bryan Smith, *A Spiritual Formation Workbook* (San Francisco: Harper, 1994).

10. See Norvene Vest, *Bible Reading for Spiritual Growth* (San Francisco: Harper, 1993).

11. For more information, contact Upper Room Books, 1908 Grand Ave., Nashville, TN 37202. Ask for the *Spiritual Director's Manual*.

12. For more information, contact The Parish Nurse Resource Center, 1700 Western Ave., Room 204, Park Ridge, IL 60068, 312-696-8773.

Chapter 6

1. Hans-Reudi Weber, *Living in the Image of Christ* (Valley Forge, Pa.: Judson Press, 1986), 8.

2. Maria Harris, "Questioning Lay Ministry," in *The Laity in Ministry: The Whole People of God for the Whole World*, ed. George Peck and John Hoffman (Valley Forge, Pa.: Judson Press, 1984), 37.

3. George Peck, "Reconceiving the Ministry of the Laity: A Personal Testimony," in *The Laity in Ministry: The Whole People of God for the Whole World*, ed. George Peck and John Hoffman (Valley Forge, Pa.: Judson Press, 1984), 16.

4. William Diehl, *Christianity and Real Life* (Philadelphia: Fortress Press, 1976), 34.

5. Celia Hahn, *Lay Voices in an Open Church* (Bethesda, Md.: The Alban Institute, 1985), 30.

6. Ibid., 16.

7. William Broholm, "Toward Claiming and Identifying Our Ministry in the Work Place," in *The Laity in Ministry: The Whole People of God for the Whole World*, ed. George Peck and John Hoffman (Valley Forge, Pa.: Judson Press, 1984), 151-160.

8. Carolyn MacDougall, "Toward Claiming and Identifying Our Ministry in the Work Place," in *The Laity in Ministry: The Whole People of God for the Whole World*, ed. George Peck and John Hoffman (Valley Forge, Pa.: Judson Press, 1984), 52-59.

9. Davida Foy Crabtree, *The Empowering Church* (Bethesda, Md.: The Alban Institute, 1989), 2.

10. Peck, "Reconceiving the Ministry," 17.

11. Hahn, *Lay Voices*, 34.

12. Charles Bryant, *Rediscovering Our Spiritual Gifts: Building Up the Body of Christ through the Gifts of the Spirit* (Nashville: Upper Room Books, 1991).

13. Thomas Hawkins, *Claiming God's Promises: A Guide to Discovering Your Spiritual Gifts* (Nashville: Abingdon Press, 1992).

Chapter 7

1. Jill Hudson, *Evaluating Ministry* (Bethesda, Md.: The Alban Institute, 1992), 8.

2. Ibid., 64.

3. Ibid., 21-38.

4. William R. Nelson, *Ministry Formation for Effective Leadership* (Nashville: Abingdon Press, 1988).

5. Jackson Carroll, Carl Dudley, and William McKinney, eds., *Handbook for Congregational Studies* (Nashville: Abingdon Press, 1986), 115-118.

6. The *Guide for Continuing Growth* is the property of the Academy of Parish Clergy, 13500 Shaker Blvd., #601, Cleveland, OH 44120.

7. Lloyd Edwards, *How We Belong, Fight, and Pray: The MBTI as a Key to Congregational Dynamics* (Bethesda, Md.: The Alban Institute, 1993).

Chapter 8

1. For more information, see Roy Oswald and Otto Kroeger, *Personality Type and Religious Leadership* (Bethesda, Md.: The Alban Institute, 1988); Lloyd Edwards, *How We Belong, Fight, and Pray: The MBTI as a Key to Congregational Dynamics* (Bethesda, Md.: The Alban Institute, 1993).

2. Joey Faucette, "Pastoral Wholeness: Preaching and Teaching That Heals," *Congregations* (November-December 1983): 11-12.

Chapter 9

1. Herbert Simon, "The Architecture of Complexity," *Proceedings of the American Philosophical Society* 106, no. 6 (1962): 469.

2. Karl Weick, *The Social Psychology of Organizing* (Reading, Mass.: Addison-Wesley, 1979), 69-88.

3. Charles Somervill, *Leadership Strategies for Ministers* (Philadelphia: Westminster Press, 1987), 105.

4. Roy Oswald, *Power Analysis of a Congregation* (Bethesda, Md.: The Alban Institute, 1981).

BIBLIOGRAPHY

Berk, Richard and Peter Rossi. *Thinking about Program Evaluation.* Newbury Park, Calif.: Sage, 1990.

Broholm, William. "Toward Claiming and Identifying Our Ministry in the Work Place." In *The Laity in Ministry: The Whole People of God for the Whole World*, edited by George Peck and John Hoffman, 149-160. Valley Forge, Pa.: Judson Press, 1984.

Bryant, Charles. *Rediscovering Our Spiritual Gifts: Building Up the Body of Christ through the Gifts of the Spirit.* Nashville: Upper Room Books, 1991.

Buttry, Daniel. *Bringing Your Church Back to Life.* Valley Forge, Pa.: Judson Press, 1988.

Carroll, Jackson, Carl Dudley, and William McKinney, eds. *Handbook for Congregational Studies.* Nashville: Abingdon Press, 1986.

Crabtree, Davida Foy. *The Empowering Church.* Bethesda, Md.: The Alban Institute, 1989.

Diehl, William. *Christianity and Real Life.* Philadelphia, Pa.: Fortress Press, 1976.

Dudley, Carl S. and Sally A. Johnson. *Energizing the Congregation: Images That Shape Your Church's Ministry.* Louisville: Westminster/John Knox Press, 1993.

Edwards, Lloyd. *How We Belong, Fight, and Pray.* Bethesda, Md.:
The Alban Institute, 1993.

Faucette, Joey. "Pastoral Wholeness: Preaching and Teaching That
Heals." *Congregations,* November-December 1983, 10-13.

Fothergill, Donald. "A Leader's Manual for Renewing Mainline
Churches." D.Min. project,Fuller Theological Seminary, 1982.

Fruend, John, Frank Williams, and Benjamin Perles. *Elementary Business Statistics: The Modern Approach.* Englewood Cliffs, N.J.:
Prentice-Hall, 1993.

Guba, Egon, and Yvonna S. Lincoln. *Effective Evaluation.* San
Francisco: Jossey-Bass, 1983.

Guide for Continuing Growth, Academy of Parish Clergy, 13500 Shaker
Blvd., #601, Cleveland, OH 44120.

Hahn, Celia. *Lay Voices in an Open Church.* Bethesda, Md.: The
Alban Institute, 1985.

Harris, Maria. "Questioning Lay Ministry." In *The Laity in Ministry:
The Whole People of God for the Whole World,* edited by George
Peck and John Hoffman, 33-46. Valley Forge, Pa.: Judson Press,
1984.

Hawkins, Thomas. *Claiming God's Promises: A Guide to Discovering
Your Spiritual Gifts.* Nashville: Abingdon Press, 1992.

Hudson, Jill. *Evaluating Ministry.* Bethesda, Md.: The Alban Institute,
1992.

Laubach, David C. *The Good News Link* 13 (1990): 1-4. (This is a
newsletter of Board of National Ministries, American Baptist
Churches, USA).

MacDougall, Carolyn. "Toward Claiming and Identifying Our Ministry in the Work Place." In *The Laity in Ministry: The Whole People of God for the Whole World*, edited by George Peck and John Hoffman, 49-62. Valley Forge, Pa.: Judson Press, 1984.

Maxam, Donald. "The Church Renewal Movement in Sociological Perspective." *Review of Religious Research* 23, no. 2 (1981): 195-204.

McIntosh, Duncan and Richard Rusbuldt. *Planning Growth in Your Church*. Valley Forge, Pa.: Judson Press, 1983.

Mead, Loren. *Evaluation of, by, for, and to the Clergy*. Bethesda, Md.: The Alban Institute, 1977.

Mead, Loren. *More Than Numbers: The Ways Churches Grow*. Bethesda, Md.: The Alban Institute, 1993.

Mead, Loren. *The Once and Future Church*. Bethesda, Md.: The Alban Institute, 1991.

Nelson, William R. *Ministry Formation for Effective Leadership*. Nashville: Abingdon Press, 1988.

Olsen, Charles M. "Research: What Makes Church Boards Work? Part I: Why Do Church Board Members Burn Out?" *Congregations*, May-June 1993, 10-12.

Olsen, Charles M. "Research: What Makes Church Boards Work? Part II: Church Boards as Spiritual Leaders." *Congregations*, July-August 1993, 16-18.

Oswald, Roy and Speed Leas. *The Inviting Church*. Bethesda, Md.: The Alban Institute, 1987.

Oswald, Roy and Otto Kroeger. *Personality Type and Religious Leadership*. Bethesda, Md.: The Alban Institute, 1988.

Oswald, Roy. *Power Analysis of a Congregation.* Bethesda, Md.: The Alban Institute, 1981.

Owens, Owen D. *Covenant Prayer Group Manual.* Valley Forge, Pa.: Church and Community Development, American Baptist Churches, USA, 1988.

Packer, James I. "Steps to the Renewal of the Christian People." In *Summons to Faith and Renewal,* edited by Peter S. Williamson and Kevin Perrotta. Ann Arbor: Servant Books, 1983.

Parish Nurse Resource Center, 1700 Western Ave. Room 204, Park Ridge, IL 60068.

Peck, George. "Reconceiving the Ministry of the Laity: A Personal Testimony." In *The Laity in Ministry, The Whole People of God for the Whole World,* edited by George Peck and John Hoffman, 13-19. Valley Forge, Pa.: Judson Press, 1984.

Peters, Thomas and Robert Waterman. *In Search of Excellence: Lessons from America's Best Run Companies.* New York: Harper & Row, 1982.

Schaller, Lyle. *The Local Church Looks to the Future.* Nashville: Abingdon Press, 1968.

Scriven, Michael. "Pros and Cons about Goal-Free Evaluation," *Evaluation Comment* (1974): 1-4.

Simon, Herbert. "The Architecture of Complexity." *Proceedings of the American Philosophical Society* 106 (1962): 467-482.

Smith, James Bryan. *A Spiritual Formation Workbook.* San Francisco: Harper, 1994.

Snyder, Howard. *Signs of the Spirit: How God Reshapes the Church.* Grand Rapids: Zondervan, 1989.

Somervill, Charles. *Leadership Strategies for Ministers.* Philadelphia: Westminster Press, 1987.

Stake, R. E. *Evaluating the Arts in Education: A Responsive Approach.* Columbus, Ohio: Merrill, 1975.

Stufflebeam, D. L., et al. *Educational Evaluation and Decision-Making.* Itasca, Ill.: Peacock, 1971.

Tyler, Ralph. *Basic Principles of Curriculum and Instruction.* Chicago: University of Chicago Press, 1950.

Vest, Norvene. *Bible Reading for Spiritual Growth.* San Francisco: Harper, 1993.

Wagner, Peter. *Leading Your Church to Growth.* Ventura, Calif.: Regal, 1984.

Weber, Hans-Reudi. *Living in the Image of Christ.* Valley Forge, Pa.: Judson Press, 1986.

Weick, Karl. *The Social Psychology of Organizing.* Reading, Mass.: Addison-Wesley, 1979.

Woods, C. Jeff. "A Long Range Planning Primer." *The Clergy Journal,* March 1992, 20-22.

Woods, C. Jeff. "Surveying to Find a Church's Distinctiveness." *Christian Ministry,* January-February 1991, 11-14.

253
W894

90457

LINCOLN CHRISTIAN COLLEGE AND SEMINARY

33220832

253 W894
Woods, Charles Jeffrey,
 1958-
User friendly evaluation

DEMCO

3 4711 00085 8789